orders at
www.FacultyFables.com

visit
http://GeraldStone.posterous.com

To Don,
mentor and friend
whose advice set my
path on the road to
meeting all these odd
characters.

Gerald

Faculty Fables:
A Campy Exposé

By Gerald C. Stone

With illustrations assembled by Berni

*"If you feel that you have both feet planted on solid ground,
then the university has failed you."*
– Robert Goheen

"The University brings out all abilities including incapability."
– Anton Chekhov

Library of Congress Cataloging-in-Publication Data.
Stone, Gerald Cory
　　　　Faculty Fables / Gerald C. Stone
　　　　ISBN 978-0-615-44862-6
　　　　1. Humor–College.　　I. Title: Faculty fables.
　　　　　　　　　　　　　　II. Title: Faculty fables: A campy exposé.

©Copyright Gerald C. Stone 2011.

Published in the United States in 2011 by Chautauqua Press LLC.

Berni Pincus, illustrator
Leah Lirely, editor

No part of this book may be reproduced by any mechanical, photographic, or electronic process, or in the form of a phonographic recording, nor may it be stored in a retrieval system, transmitted, or otherwise copied for public or private use, without written permission from the publisher.

Printed in the United States of America by A&A Printing, Tampa, Fla.

First U.S. printing 2011.

Chautauqua Press LLC
11925 Mont Lake Drive
Boynton Beach, Florida 33437-4918

Contents

Preface i
1- Voices 1
2- General Education 6
3- Food Stains 11
4- Sharks 14
5- Ethical Dilemmas 18
6- Class Reading 23
7- Excuses 27
8- Dorm Petting 31
9- Dreams 35
10- 3.0 Grading 39
11- Tricks 43
12- Learning Center 47
13- Logic I 51
14- Counselors 55
15- Grad Teaching Assistants 59
16- Grad TAs, the sequel 63
17- Insecure 67
18- Evaluations 71
19- The Scholar 75
20- Dumb 79
21- Consultants 83
22- The Secret 88
23- 6th Period 93
24- Big Words 97
25- Enrollment 101
26- Publish 105
27- Quantitative Grading 109
28- Majors 113
29- Modern History 117
30- Audio-Visual 122
31- Red-Ink Grading 126
32- Endowments 130
33- Toughies 135
34- Writing Requirement 139
35- The Tell 143
36- Arrogance, part 1 148
37- Arrogance, part 2 153

Preface

What's a preface in a humor book going to say: This book is funny? And who bothers to read prefaces anyway? Especially those in textbooks that give the author's credentials, make verbose attempts to say why this text is different from (and better than) competing work, and continue for three pages thanking every colleague the faculty member ever knew in hopes they all adopt the book for their courses. No, I'm just not going to embarrass myself by sinking to that level of pandering.

Although, perhaps a little background is necessary. *Faculty Fables: A Campy Exposé* offers an insider's revelations about the idiosyncrasies of college teachers, administrators and students, and lends just enough truth to be discomforting. I began writing it in the early 1980s as a humor column for the op-ed pages of college newspapers. I hoped to syndicate the series and actually did sell it widely across the United States to five campus papers.

I was a young journalism professor then and fortunate the column fizzled out because, without having to divulge authoring such clandestine nonsense, I started advancing through the echelons of academic administration. I rose from scholarly researcher to department chair to distinguished visiting professor to graduate studies director to college dean. The higher I climbed, the more closet-skeleton material I easily collected to write about and kept churning out these little essays right up to today. I apologize for not becoming a chancellor.

Don't worry about context for the earlier pieces. I've updated everything. For example, my brief reference to gladiator-type films previously used Charlton Heston but now names Russell Crowe; computers replace typewriters; a sizable endowment is $20 million rather than $250,000; eight-tracks are replaced by CDs. That ought to suffice.

But most of the examples will never change:

• Dr. Wanda Funderbinder, who needed to publish for

tenure but was in danger of ending her career by becoming a superior classroom teacher;
- the clerk who grew his tiny campus Learning Center into its own major university;
- a professor so notorious about refusing excuses that students waited after the bell in case a classmate was dumb enough to try;
- Dr. Wedgewood Thornblatt, who foolishly made the mistake of reviewing a multiple-choice exam in class merely to improve student learning;
- guidance counselors: The years spent in college are proportional to the number of conferences;
- foods teachers spill while grading papers;
- Peter Primrose, whose students took cruel advantage of his nostalgic sentiments;
- the golden rule of academic administration: When in doubt, overreact;
- The Secret to college success is reading what your professors have written;
- Smitty Penderghast, who increased enrollments by rejecting the best student applicants;
- and a cornucopia of other eccentric and misplaced souls who haunt the hallowed halls of academia.

When you finish *Faculty Fables,* you undoubtably will be asking yourself, "What small favor can I do for this great humor writer in return for the hours of enjoyment I've received?" That's easy. Encourage all your colleagues to buy the book.

You can tell them you were my inspiration.

Fable 1 – Voices

Faculty members – you may already have noticed this – are not like other people. Part of their problem deals with the way they are paid. They receive an annual salary but work only nine months a year, actually seven-and-a-half if you exclude winter vacation and fall and spring breaks. Worse yet, the weekly 6-to-12 class hour schedule changes erratically every semester. And then there's "dead week" when students prepare for finals and professors just sort of mill around waiting to hand out the exams.

So it is difficult for faculty members to associate the actual time they put in with the pay they receive. People who work 9-to-5 jobs also find it hard to associate faculty members' pay with the hours faculty members put in, but that concern exceeds the scope of this presentation.

Dr. Fenwick Pettipotter was pushing 60, just at that dangerous age when a normally absent-minded professor runs the risk of becoming an abnormally absent-minded professor. It happened to Pettipotter one morning as he engaged in the bane of all faculty rituals. He was late to class and still circling the campus looking for a parking space.

A business ethics teacher, Pettipotter displayed a keen sense of self-righteous indignation about his lot. The lot about which he was particularly indignant, the only one with vacancies at 8:30 a.m., was a mile from his office. It made him furious every morning as he circled looking for a better space. He muttered, cursed, grit his teeth and often shouted out loud during these futile vehicular vigils.

On this particular morning, he yelled, "They don't pay me to circle the campus looking for a parking space!" And then it happened. He thought at first he heard himself answering himself, not an unusual occurrence. But the voice was a deep, resonant bass, a god-like voice or perhaps James Earl Jones, and it said, "Wrong you are, Fenwick. They DO pay you to circle the

Dr. Pettipotter yelled, "They don't pay me to circle the campus looking for a parking space!" And then it happened.

campus looking for a parking space. That is exactly what they are paying you for right now."

Pettipotter slammed on his brakes and skidded to the curb. "That's right," he thought. "They are paying me to circle the campus!"

"Yes," the voice said, "and you have been cheating them when you give up easily and walk the mile to class."

"Well, I rarely find a closer space …."

"That's beside the point," the voice chided. "If they pay you to circle the campus for a space, then you need to circle more. Take the next hour."

"But I'm late for class now."

"What are they paying you for?" the voice asked.

That settled it. Dr. Pettipotter skipped his class and spent the next hour circling the campus looking for a closer space. He passed up two of them because his hour hadn't elapsed. He finally found a space only two blocks from his office and hummed pleasantly as he walked in.

For two weeks thereafter, he spent at least an hour a day circling the campus looking for a close parking space.

Dr. Pettipotter was daydreaming in his office when it occurred to him that if they paid him to circle the campus, what else did they actually pay him to do that he might not be doing enough? He spent a lot of time in boring committee meetings, in listening to undergraduates' love life worries during office hours and in drinking coffee while talking to colleagues in the faculty lounge. Was he also paid to do these things?

"Darn right you are, Fenwick." The voice again. It had been lurking behind the filing cabinet waiting for an opening. "Spend more time in the bathroom."

"I've missed you," Pettipotter confessed.

"I'll call when you need me," the voice said reassuringly.

And from that time forward, Dr. Pettipotter could be seen talking to someone who was not there.

Of course, Pettipotter wasn't the only faculty member who did that. Far from it. He had merely joined the ranks of many of his colleagues who spoke to walls and lectured out the window.

He could have continued in that manner for years, no one the wiser, had it not been for the annual campus-wide faculty meeting.

Dr. Pettipotter shuffled into the auditorium and sat with his department members and chairman. The voice had been particularly active during the past week, far more outspoken and controlling.

Just before the university president closed the half-hour meeting, she asked rhetorically if anybody had any questions.

"On your feet, Fenwick," the voice demanded. "Don't let her get away with it!"

Dr. Pettipotter rose to the astonishment of the assembly and said, "Madam President, I fear you are shortchanging the university by ending this important meeting early."

"You tell 'em, Fenwick," the voice prompted.

"Beg your pardon?" the president said.

"We work hard to earn our pay at this school …"

"Atta boy," the voice egged him on.

"… and a measly half-hour doesn't do justice to our salaries."

"Dr. Pettipotter, you want me to continue the meeting?"

"Absolutely. We meet only once a year, and since we're paid good money to convene here, integrity demands that we devote the proper time."

"Now drive it home!" urged the voice.

"Let's earn our pay today by extending the meeting until nightfall. I'm sure everyone is eager to give proper deliberation in exchange for the salaries we receive."

Pettipotter continued in this vein for a few moments goaded on by his unseen voice until the provost came to the microphone and declared the meeting adjourned.

In the 9-to-5 job world, Pettipotter's diatribe would have earned early retirement or a public pillorying. But the world of tenured academia deals with dissidents in a more subtle manner.

The president hadn't quite understood the nuances of Pettipotter's remarks but recognized his outburst had something to do with the always-sensitive issue of faculty salaries and work hours, which he apparently wanted to discuss openly. She authorized his department chair to give him a nice raise, his first raise in five years, just to appease him, and to forbid him from attending all future group gatherings on campus, especially hers.

"No group meetings at all?" the chairman had asked. "You mean no classes either?"

"I don't want him talking to ANY groups," the president said. "Let him circle the damn parking lots for all I care."

§

Fable 2 – General Education

Universities grapple today with what perhaps has always been higher education's most fundamental question. It is none other than defining the purpose of a college, and it focuses on the general education requirements each institution demands of all students. Perhaps a moment's background would be helpful.

During many of the last 60 years, higher education has moved curricula toward career preparation. The development evolved over the decades as universities became more available to all people. Previously, high schools and technical schools prepared citizens for the work force, while universities prepared them for binge drinking and ingrained a propensity for asking strangers at parties where they graduated.

But modern society now insists on a college degree for what were formerly considered "the trades," such as nursing, bookkeeping, drafting, criminal justice and journalism, to name only a few. Today's students probably can't fathom how someone could become, say, a politician or even a local television news anchor without having a college education, but this once was so.

Some have said a college education today bears little resemblance to the classic ideal of producing a liberally educated, thinking individual. Others say this is hockey-puck mentality. They counter that if a student insists on learning for the sake of self-improvement alone, with no practical outcome whatsoever, "Let them go get a Ph.D. and teach college."

Regardless of extreme positions, broader general education requirements are destined for approval, particularly at our "emerging" institutions, which seek the same academic credibility as those institutions that emerged more than 100 years ago and couldn't care less about general education requirements.

Two former classmates seemed to epitomize all the virtues

and pitfalls of the present general education debate.

Lance Bowman was the zenith of the "classic" educational ideal. He believed learning was an end in itself. The young man triple-majored in Latin, biology and astronomy. He was an avid reader, head cheerleader, a member of the debate team, chess club, the university chorus and two fraternities (one under an assumed name as the two houses were constantly playing pranks on one another ... Lance once had to sneak into a second-story window and blow himself up with a large firecracker while he was sound asleep in his cot).

Although he was graduated with more than 300 credits, his transcript was actually much longer since he repeated many courses to achieve his ambition of graduating with a solid "B" average.

Charming, dapper and urbane, Lance livened every party as he recited Horatio and accompanied himself on the slide trombone in Dixieland tempo. He stayed abreast of current events and avoided correcting people's spoken grammar or mispronunciations.

As the classically educated graduate, he never questioned what field he would go into. He became an encyclopedia salesman, married, had five children, lived in the suburbs and attended the few cultural events he could afford.

Ever grateful to his alma mater, Lance faithfully attended all graduations as a member of the audience. Showing support was the most he could do for his university, and during one of these graduations he witnessed the shameful downfall of his former classmate, one Elbert Dipstik.

Dipstik marched to a different drum in college – a monotonic cadence. He was a math major who had graduated high school early, just after entering puberty.

As a gifted lad, he qualified for the university's special curriculum. He took none of the general education requirements as he scored into advanced trig as a freshman. All of his classes were math classes, and he was the star pupil in each.

He was graduated at age 17 and became a statistician in a brokerage house. While the firm paid him handsomely, his talents were such that he developed formulas in his spare time for IBM, Google, government employee retirement funds and Las Vegas casinos. He retained rights on all these formulae and retired wealthy at age 32.

Despite his career success, Dipstik had no friends, played no sports, had no hobbies and spent a lot of time rearranging his socks drawer. His bookshelves were empty. He enjoyed watching television but knew he wasn't very good at it.

He liked frozen dinners and spent countless hours selecting them in the grocery store. For a really big treat he attended craft shows in the walkways of malls where he examined leather belts and beaded bracelets. He listened intently to computer-generated surveys he occasionally received by phone and found if he didn't hang up, the message would be repeated as long as he could stay awake.

Unfortunately, the development director at Dipstik's alma mater got wind of his extensive financial holdings and determined to get a large donation. Dipstik was asked to deliver the commencement address at the next graduation. The thought petrified him. What did a math major know of the world? He had nothing to say, and since he hadn't taken speech in college, he knew he would not say it well. He spent many sleepless nights scribbling notes he could not decipher.

Commencement day found him on the riser in black gown and mortarboard. He was called to the rostrum by the university chancellor. Silence fell on the assembly.

"My friends," he began, but the words were shrill and frightened him into an exaggerated pause which at length filled the auditorium with nervous audience mumblings. He drew on all his courage and forced out the words:

$$< 7 \times 3.3 \log \frac{(1i - 1)^2}{N + 5r \ (X * 610)}$$

The audience was struck to dumbfounded silence, which Dipstik misinterpreted as an improvement, so he continued:

"My friends," he began, but the words were shrill and frightened him into an exaggerated pause.

$$E(A' + a(1/2 - 13))$$
$$\text{intgr. b....bi } \{814 \, . \, ^\wedge m\} + U'$$

which he reduced to its smallest possible fraction and continued along the same vein for another half hour until even the assembled math faculty fell asleep.

At the end he fled the auditorium in humiliation. "Oh," he thought, "if only I had been forced to take some liberal arts classes in college." But, alas, it was too late. Dipstik was marked with the public shame of his narrow perspective.

Rumor has it he is hiding away either at his villa on the Italian coast (the one decorated with paintings of jungle animals on black velvet) or on his yacht in Puget Sound, the "My Boat."

§

Fable 3 – Food Stains

In the continuing spirit of demystifying that austere personage, the College Professor, allow me to share my treatise: "Foods I Have Spilled on Student Papers."

Now I'm not referring to anything so mundane as teachers dripping coffee on student papers when answering the phone. That hardly counts, and any student who would make an issue of such a routine occurrence deserves the appropriate remembrance when term grades are calculated. I'm talking real food stains: avocado dip or cheesecake.

Knowledgeable students easily discern telltale spilled food signs by a stain and slight crumpling in a specific region of the returned paper. A stainless paper crumpled uniformly across the entire sheet is more likely to have been thrown in the trash basket once during the grading process, perhaps by mistake.

But having your paper thrown in the trash during grading is something that has probably happened to everyone. The real issue here is exotic food stains dropped on student papers.

There was the time a set of papers got wedged into my briefcase compartment adjacent to a not-so-carefully wrapped bologna sandwich on white bread with lettuce and dijon mustard. I had forgotten that morning when making the sandwich that I had a luncheon engagement, so the briefcase remained in the locked car under 96-degree temperatures for about four hours. Not quite long enough to cook the bologna, the heat only caused the waxed paper to unravel. The edge of each student paper was sautéed in dijon, and one paper benefited additionally from the wilted lettuce.

Small potatoes? I thought so, too, so I graded them and turned them back without a word … nor was a word raised.

One other major incident involved soup: borsch actually, with whole beets and carrots. Our cat jumped on the table, and I knocked the bowl over as I swatted at her playfully with my trusty sickle. Luckily, the extensive red-ink grading marks

Luckily, the borsch mess was disguised by the extensive red-ink grading marks already on the papers.

already on the papers disguised the borsch mess. I handed their papers back and apologized to students about my leaky pen.

Most people have a weakness for some special food. Mine happens to be all kinds of desserts, with heaps of whipped cream, any time from noon through bedtime, and taco-flavored Doritos. Unfortunately, I can no longer indulge in the latter because of repetitive heartburn and the inability to find them on grocery shelves. Today's Doritos bags boast taco with cheddar cheese, and the two flavors together couldn't interest me less.

But back to the whipped cream. I have found it nearly impossible to write on a whipped cream-stained paper with any writing implement yet invented. No marks stick to whipped cream. Should a student seek the novelty of having a paper returned without a single red mark on it, just spread whipped cream across the surface and blot lightly before turning in the paper. I am horrified when I consider the numbers of students who have graduated because of my penchant for desserts.

Be wary of eating candy bars while grading. Nibbling a Baby Ruth and dropping chocolate shavings runs the risk of exceeding the barrier of good taste. Such stains might be interpreted as commentary on the quality of a student's work. Likewise with orange juice or lemonade.

Is there a teacher who never left a coffee mug or teacup ring on a student's paper? I doubt it. And after a massive grading weekend, one would expect the last several papers to be subject to cognac spills or vodka sloshes, along with the obligatory hot-pepper cheese and cracker-crumb smudges.

But the coup de grace of food stains has to be the time I was eating smoked oysters with a toothpick from a tin while grading papers. It is astounding to realize a day later that the offensive odor permeating the entire office and extending halfway down the hall of the building can be attributed to a single drop of smoked oyster oil on one paper in one stack on a professor's desk. The power of that briny sea smell surprised even me, and I'm sure the student who had that paper returned never realized why he left class humming, "I'm Popeye the sailor man …."

§

Fable 4 – Sharks

I once met a college professor who had never taken an education course. He divulged his confession with little actual pride, although many education majors told him he hadn't missed much. Still, he wondered if some aspect of his own teaching might be improved had he been through a course in how to teach.

Colleagues told him not to worry, but they neglected to tell him about the Shark Syndrome, and Wedgewood Thorenblatt had to learn the hard way in the great frothing vortex of the lecture hall.

Now, it is not clear if the Shark Syndrome is some sort of initiation ritual that teachers experience and then remain mum about because they believe all new faculty members deserve to experience it for themselves. Perhaps teachers are too embarrassed to share this happening with anyone. But in the interest of further illuminating the college experience, I will describe the Shark Syndrome just as Thorenblatt related it to me the evening of the day it happened to him.

Weggie Thorenblatt had been a college teacher about three years and he took an unusually active, almost unique, interest in the educational welfare of his students. He wanted them to learn something in his classes. Though he had not taken an education course himself, he was concerned about the pedagogic paradigm and began to worry that the multiple-choice tests he gave in his 200-plus student Intro to Visual Arts lecture classes were not really serving their educational purpose.

"I just give them the exams, run the answer sheets through the computer and post the scores in the room," he thought," and they never really know what they missed unless they come to my office to look over the test, which I urge them to do, but which they never do unless they either fail the test miserably or they ace it. In neither instance is learning served."

He came up with the solution that every new instructor hits

upon, and which is his or her undoing. He would pass out the test forms in class and go over the answers. "Gee," he thought, "this will be great. Not only will I not have to prepare a lecture that day, but I will be able to explain to them why their answers were wrong and which answers were right. They will learn from their mistakes!" But the only one who would learn that day was Weggie himself.

It took 15 minutes to distribute the forms to each student in the hall. Then Thorenblatt began the review. He was doing well. He would just call out the right answer for those questions missed by only a few, but for those questions missed by many he would explain in some detail why the right multiple-choice answer was right and all the other choices wrong. Halfway through the review, he noticed a hand held high in the middle of the room.

"You have a question about this one?" he asked aloud.

"Yes, Dr. Thorenblatt. You asked if Picasso is known most for being: a. an Impressionist; b. a Cubist; c. a Constructivist; d. an Abstractionist; or e. a dirty old man. I thought you were asking how most people in the world would think of Picasso, and so I answered 'e. a dirty old man' since he was very old and since the lewd art he did in his early years brought him so much attention."

"You interpreted this question as a general question about how most people in the world would think of Picasso?"

"Yes."

"And you knew about his licentious paintings and his longevity?"

"Yes."

"Well, I guess if that's how you interpreted the question, I could give you credit for that one. See me after class."

A second hand shot up, and it didn't wait for recognition.

"Dr. Thorenblatt, the same thing happened to me. I knew about his early pornography and how long he lived."

Thorenblatt was surprised. "All right," he said, "you see me after class too."

Three shouts from different parts of the room followed

"How many people in the room missed that question, and how many got 'e. a dirty old man'?"

with varying exclamations about age, debauchery and misinterpretation.

"Now, wait just a minute," Thorenblatt said. "How many people in the room missed that question?"

Forty-two hands went up.

"And how many got 'e. a dirty old man'?"

All hands remained aloft.

"Put down your hands if you didn't know Picasso painted nudes and lived into his 90s."

All hands remained aloft. Thorenblatt was cornered. "Okay," he said, "see me after class if your hand is still up now." And grins appeared as the tension ebbed.

"Dr. Thorenblatt," a youth called out from the back of the room, "I have a question about number 16."

"We've already been over number 16."

"Yes, but I misinterpreted it when you asked what color had no rhyme. I knew there was no rhyme for 'orange' but I thought you meant 'rind' and since an orange has a rind and a yellow lemon has a rind, I said it was 'blue' that had no rind and you counted it wrong."

Thorenblatt was speechless, and the class welcomed his silence as further weakness.

Hands and shouts sprang up from all over the room as a chorus of complaints aired in unison. Once they had smelled blood, the sharks were beyond control, and Thorenblatt spent the rest of the class period in futile thrashing at the oncoming jaws. He was a quivering, jelly-like hulk when the bell rang. It was all he could do to have students sign a roster of grade corrections on their way out.

A colleague found him mumbling gibberish in the front row of the lecture hall and asked what had happened. Thorenblatt provided only the highlights and the man said, "Oh, the Shark Syndrome."

He helped Thorenblatt out of the room, which had to be cleared for his Higher Education Methods and Practices class that met the next hour.

§

Fable 5 – Ethical Dilemmas

Who is charged with upholding the ethical conduct of a university? Why, none other than the high administration of that university.

Faced with an ethical dilemma involving students or faculty, the high administration adheres to a single golden rule in every situation: When in doubt, overreact. It's the only way the university can maintain ethical standards and appear totally without moral compromise before local civic groups and the press. So important is the golden rule of ethical conduct, it deserves some serious treatment here.

Note the case of Sorghum State, one of those Southern schools of the "emerging" genre. "Emerging" universities are those still building their reputations. For some reason, already emerged universities don't adhere to the golden rule of ethics with the same devotion as emerging schools. But who am I to call them on it?

Sorghum was an up-and-coming school with a former military man as its president (the only better choice is a former governor). He was Col. John Thwartmire, known as "Old Butt and Snort Thwartmire" in the last war because he disdained subtlety. His fellow officers used to say, "When wiser heads forbear, Old Butt and Snort is right in there." His present aides at Sorghum were Dr. Twiddledee and Dr. Twiddledumb, the vice presidents of academics and administration respectively.

Sorghum had faced impending disaster some years before when a fraternity hosted a togaless party after a major volleyball victory. The scene that Saturday night had been mayhem at best, and nearly 20 members of the frat house and their sorority dates were facing charges by church time Sunday morning. A meeting was held later that day. It went something like this:

Dr. Twiddledee told Col. Thwartmire the news. "Hang them all," Col. Thwartmire said. "The reputation of the regiment is at stake."

"But, sir," Dr. Twiddledumb protested, "They are the cream of this school's Greek system and the offspring of some of our wealthiest alumni."

Col. Thwartmire listened to the advice of his vice presidents. He decided to forego the execution, against his better judgment, and merely banned all fraternities and sororities from the campus for five years. Some said the administration's response to the situation was too harsh, but the university's image was at stake. The golden rule prevailed.

The next year brought the big computer scandal. Four professors had begun a consulting business and were using the university computer to keep books and analyze business records for local firms.

"Draw and quarter them," Col. Thwartmire said. "Leave their bones to bleach in the sun as an example to others. Hold their children until their families make full repayment of our computer time."

"Begging your pardon, Col. Thwartmire," Dr. Twiddledee said, "but they use that business data to publish research on those companies' management trends. There's a narrow ethical question here."

Col. Thwartmire again abided by the advice of his vice presidents. He closed the computer center to students and faculty as a warning to future academic entrepreneurs.

The next year witnessed the "review-of-campus-restroom-stall-doodles" article in the student newspaper, always an embarrassing moment in the annals of college journalism with the attendant phone calls from the dean of women, the mayor and various large donors. Col. Thwartmire was livid.

"Wash out their mouths with lye. Lash and publicly brand them. Guillotine their typing fingers. Padlock their presses!"

"But sir," Dr. Twiddledumb advised, "the First Amendment guarantees freedom of expression to college newspapers. We can't shut them down."

Col. Thwartmire conceded, but he replaced their newsprint with rolls of tissue paper, bought a special smearing ink, and made the dean of women copy reader and censor. To stymie

Col. Thwartmire was livid.
"Wash out their mouths with lye. Lash and publicly brand them. Guillotine their typing fingers!"

campus readership he changed the paper's name to "Yankee Rag."

Later that same year a civic group, the Great Granddaughters of the Grandsons of the Spanish American War, confirmed a rumor that nude models were being used in art classes. Col. Thwartmire banned art education from the university, closed the department and leased the space. "Those are probably the same people who spray-painted graffiti on the parking lot," he said, and he had a stadium built on the lot to prevent a similar incident of vandalism.

"When it comes to ethics," he told his two Twiddles, "there can be no compromise."

The next year witnessed the big cheating scandal. Five law school students turned in papers written by one of those online essay writing firms and were caught when teachers noticed the papers were vastly superior to these students' in-class work.

Col. Thwartmire had his way in the matter. He expelled the five culprits and revoked their undergraduate degrees (in case they had cheated there also). The president wrote a lengthy letter-to-the-editor of the local newspaper deploring the situation and naming all the students involved. He invited the state bar association to review the credentials of all practicing attorneys holding Sorghum degrees. While the local legal community was outraged, the ethical fiber of Sorghum remained intact.

The next year Col. Thwartmire faced a really serious moral dilemma when a representative of a Middle Eastern nation of the oil-rich variety offered Sorghum State a $3 million endowment to begin a Center of Terrorism Studies. Col. Thwartmire was about to accept in a press conference, but the Twiddles prevailed upon him to reconsider.

"Col. Thwartmire," they warned, "we are likely to offend a lot more folks than the $3 million warrants. Remember the golden rule of ethics," they said. So the president turned the emissary over to the feds, had all of Sorghum's foreign students and faculty deported and got extensive, favorable, regional publicity. The golden rule prevailed.

With each ethical situation – and emerging universities

seem to have many on their roller coaster ride to renown – the triumvirate judicially applied the golden rule of overreaction. And it might have continued that way until their university's image eclipsed the shadowy remembrance of its former self, had it not been for last year's little scam unearthed by the IRS when it audited Sorghum's football ticket sales.

I can think of no ethical rationale for this writer to engage in yet another review of the sordid details of that nefarious incident. Reader titillation could be the only purpose. Besides, the state prosecutor publicly documented the ticket lottery and kickbacks, the NCAA easily linked the ticket scalpers to the team and its coaches, and the media exposed the dancing girls rather thoroughly.

Col. Thwartmire called his aides together in the midnight hours. Drs. Twiddledee and Twiddledumb feared the worst but were flabbergasted when their president spoke.

"Gentlemen," he began, "this is a narrow call, and as I see it, even-handed leniency must prevail. This is, after all, the football team!"

Sorghum broke the golden rule of ethics but continued to have a winning season, despite some personnel losses through indictments.

The only edict that supersedes the golden rule of ethics is the platinum parable of winning football seasons at emerging schools. Once broken, there can be no forgiveness.

§

Fable 6 – Class Reading

You aren't reading this in class? Please put it down and look around to make sure. It offends my professorial sensitivities to think some unfortunate instructor has to tolerate a student reading something like a magazine or, much more insulting, a newspaper in class.

There's just something about a student reading a newspaper in class while a teacher is trying to teach. It's not as if the thing is an "Archie" comic that teens hide behind their textbook; a newspaper blazons in-your-face. The affront is proportionate to the size of the newspaper page and inverse to how well the student tries to hide the fact he's reading. For instance, reading a tabloid is less irksome than reading a broadsheet newspaper, particularly if the student holds the broadsheet up and sticks his head in it. Even if the broadsheet spreads out flat on the desk, it tends to drip over both sides, and there's an inordinate amount of paper crinkling when turning pages.

Worse still is the possibility that something interesting or funny might be seen. Students forget they are in class and remark out loud, "Well, gosh, would you look at that!" just as if they were reading at the breakfast table. And if they read something funny, they get the giggles in class and then everyone wants to know what's in the paper, including the teacher. I try to do my part to keep humor out of writing altogether.

Sneaking something into class to read is a high school activity everyone has done at least once just for the thrill of it. Here are two female high school students talking about just such an incident:

"I read an 'Archie' comic book during algebra class."

"No! You didn't!"

"Totally, the entire hour. Like, I hid it behind my algebra book on my desk and she never caught me."

"Get out!"

"Sure did ... right up 'til the bell rang."

"Giggle, giggle, giggle."

Now an equally sexist instant replay of two male high schoolers in the same conversation:

"I just read an 'Archie' comic book in algebra class."

"The new one where Jughead becomes team captain?"

"Yeah."

"It was awesome, dude."

"Yuck, yuck, yuck."

Obviously, very Harry High School indeed. But in college, one is expected to put the little pranks of youth behind, and for a very good reason. College teachers don't know their students by name because they are blessed with them for shorter periods of time. So teachers occasionally link a student with a mannerism or characteristic the student displays in class. I've slipped up and said things like, "Yes, Miss Kneecaps" or "You had a question, Mr. Nosedrip?"

Those incidents were mildly awkward, but others have real potential for embarrassment if a teacher associates a newspaper reader with the names teachers are likely to have uttered about him under their breath, as most are linked with expletives. When a student reads a newspaper in class, teachers begin to wonder if what they are saying is less than the most important thing in a student's life at the moment, and that is simply intolerable.

I remember an incident in our freshman history class in college. A young man had been chewing gum in the hall while reading the campus paper and had been blowing huge bubbles, as was his want, and popping them loudly to impress the women folk. Just as the entry bell rang, a bubble stuck to the newspaper and burst, leaving gum and the open newspaper stuck to the poor chap's face. He could do nothing but file into class in that peculiar state, feeling his way to his desk with his one free hand.

Unfortunately, the history class was Dr. Thelma Bimwhimple's, and she tolerated aberrant behavior with the subtlety of a seasoned drill sergeant.

"Would the student with the newspaper please put it away so we can begin?" she asked loudly.

"Would the student with the newspaper please put it away so we can begin?" Dr. Bimwhimple asked loudly.

"Mumble, mumble, mumble, Dr. Bimmumble."

"I said put down that paper, you miserable lout."

"Mumble, mumble," shake with fear.

Dr. Bimwhimple strode the length of the room. She bent before the newspaper and tore two holes in it precisely at the eyes. Sizing up the situation, she grasped newspaper, bubble gum and nose in her strong fist and jerked it away in one painful sweep.

"That's an 'F' for the day, young man," she said.

Now, it doesn't matter who that individual was, but it taught a powerful lesson to the entire assemblage about reading a newspaper in class. And it took two weeks for my face to heal, although I saved quite a bit on Clearasil during the time.

§

Fable 7 – Excuses

"I didn't get my paper in on time because …."

Students don't seem to realize that faculty have heard it all before. In fact, Creative Excuses Anonymous offers a standing $10,000 prize that has never been won because each time a faculty member submits a real zinger, the board of judges writes back, "We've heard that one before."

Excuses come in several categories: 1) heart-rending sob stories; 2) so lengthy the professor will accept the excuse just to be rid of the student; 3) so ridiculous they must be true; and 4) so lame that calling the bluff would just embarrass both parties. But it doesn't matter which excuse category you use because success depends entirely on the teacher. Some accept virtually any excuse; some accept none.

Dr. Herbert Grimsley was of the latter persuasion. So notorious was he about refusing excuses that students waited at their desks after the bell rang in case their more foolish classmates tried. One young woman hadn't heard about Grimsley's reputation.

"Sir," she began, "I would have been to class on time today if not for the trumpet section of the school band. They caught me in the alleyway behind the music building and played 'Spinning Wheel' so loudly I lost all sense of direction and went to the wrong building."

"Miss Smith," Grimsley replied, "count yourself the fourth student to use the 'Spinning Wheel' excuse this year. Do you think I was born yesterday?" he asked, his voice rising. "There aren't more than three trumpet players in any school band who can play 'Spinning Wheel' well enough to be recognized," he yelled. "You've insulted my intelligence and wasted my time! Take your 'F' and get out of my sight," he roared.

Upon quick reflection, he thought he had been too lenient, so he followed her into the hall and berated her physical appearance, her choice of outfit and the way she walked. A crowd gathered on the lawn in front of her dorm to listen as Grimsley hurled verbal abuse about Miss Smith's probable ancestry toward the 12th floor of the building.

Some students believed Grimsley's invective was only for show: Something he did to make a point with the other students in class. Occasionally, one would try offering an excuse in his office.

"Sir," a young man said as he entered his professor's office crying, "It's so good of you to talk with me despite the late paper I turned in today. You see, my grandmother is terminally ill and since my dad was fired and my mom ran off with a wrestler, I had to take granny for a transfusion but we were hit by a Mack truck on the way to the hospital … do you have a hankie?"

"Whiner!" Grimsley bellowed. "I only let you in here for one reason: to have you witness this in person." He took the student's late paper and spray-painted a large "F" on it, threw the paper on the floor, stomped on it several times and then set it afire. "There's your late paper, you sniveling milksop!"

Grimsley yelled after him in the hallway, "You can sprinkle those ashes in with your granny!"

Every year Dr. Grimsley reacted more violently to attempted excuses. This little quirk resulted in lower student evaluations, endangering his job. In a last-ditch effort to reverse the trend, some faculty colleagues pitched in and bought him a ticket to one of those weekend sensitivity retreats, the kind where you reveal your soul to complete strangers, confess your insecurities and belittle yourself publicly – the kind when one year later a former group member sees you on the beach, rushes up and gives you a bear hug, but you don't remember the person at all.

The sensitivity session did Grimsley a world of good. He was contemplating the pedals of a potted daisy he had just bought to cheer his office, when in strolled Biff Golightly, a notorious blighter, with the next attempted excuse.

"Dr. Grimsley, I missed the midterm yesterday."

"Yes, Mr. Golightly, so you did."

He was contemplating the pedals of a potted daisy he had just bought to cheer his office, when in strolled Biff Golightly.

"But it wasn't my fault, sir. I was baby sitting my kid sister and she swallowed a roach pellet. So I put her in the car to take her to the doctor and I backed over her puppy's paw ... are you all right, sir?"

Grimsley had begun to whimper softly.

"So I put the dog into the car, too, and the poor thing was yowling ...."

"The poor little thing," Grimsley muttered.

"So I dropped my sister at the doctor's and I took the puppy to the vet. They had to keep him to operate on the paw."

"And your sister?"

"They won't know 'til Friday. I felt real low on the way home, and I hardly noticed the fire at the orphanage until these three little kids and a nun stopped me in the street ...."

The story continued until Grimsley's face was buried in his hands. He moaned. His shoulders shook. Finally he cried out for Golightly to stop. He'd give him a makeup on the midterm. He'd give him an "A" in the course. He'd visit his sister in the hospital.

Golightly was stunned at the effect.

"Gee, Dr. Grimsley," he said, "I never meant to upset you so much. I was just ...."

"No, I insist! Let me bring the puppy home from the vet. I want to make a donation to the orphanage."

"Dr. Grimsley," the student stammered, "it was all an excuse. I just made it up so I could retake the exam. Don't worry about it. I'll just take my 'F.'" And Golightly left the room.

Dr. Grimsley was cured. He learned that heartfelt sensitivity worked as well as venom.

Actually, every word of Golightly's story was true, including the part about the circus clowns whose tiny car had been stolen while they were doing a benefit show at the drug abuse treatment center. But Golightly had been warned by other students not to offer an excuse to Dr. Grimsley, and they had been right. The man just didn't handle excuses well.

§

Fable 8 – Dorm Petting

We hear so much these days of scandalous behavior in the dormitories, but in truth dorm petting has decreased measurably in recent years. Seldom if ever does one hear of a student harboring a pet in the dormitory.

Oh, there's the occasional snake or armadillo, but these cuddly creatures are no more than ornaments … stuffed Teddy bears, as it were. The days of dorm petting are definitely on the wane.

A classic example was Alphonse Dennizen, the "straight-A" student who later received a scholarship to Dartmouth's graduate school. He had a pet leopard with a most disquieting growl. He took "Killer" (as he fondly called the big cat) to all his classes, especially when a test paper was being returned.

Alphonse maintained a most commendable record throughout his schooling. He was graduated magna cum laude, elected president of the student body and usually took his place as first in line at the cafeteria, particularly when they served meat. Alphonse took Killer along when he went for his Dartmouth entrance interview.

Another case was Rosy Chatsworth who took her pet kangaroo to class. She never had to carry a purse, and her crib sheets were always easily accessible. But her romantic relationships were short-lived because the roo was overly protective of Rosy, plus it made a fool of itself at dances.

I had a disastrous roommate during my freshman year. He had been called Stupid Sidney back in grammar school and, through some quirk of fate, the nickname hung on.

Sidney led a miserable existence in high school. Prophetically, the single caption under his junior picture in the yearbook marked his prolonged career there: "Most likely to be here for the 10th class reunion."

The turning point of Sidney's life came during our freshman year. He went to the pet store and purchased a trained flea, the

When Professor Lemley asked for a volunteer to interpret a particularly difficult symbolic passage from the *Iliad*, Sophie could remain silent no longer.

most intelligent animal I have ever known. She was named Sophocles but, as Sidney couldn't pronounce Sophocles, he called the flea Sophie. She was beautiful, refined and very well read. Throughout their first few weeks together, Sophie displayed many other talents as an eloquent orator, a superb typist, and she played a fine game of billiards.

One day, Sidney put Sophie in his ear, as was his custom, and took his pet to his Introduction to Classics class. Sidney had warned her not to talk, but when Professor Lemley asked for a volunteer to interpret a particularly difficult symbolic passage from the *Iliad*, Sophie could remain silent no longer. She delivered from memory, through Sidney, the thesis of a short essay she had written for the old *Western Journal of Literature* some years earlier.

Amazed, Dr. Lemley called Sidney before the class. He kissed him on both cheeks (a near catastrophe for Sophie) and apologized for failing him at midterm.

Soon word got around that Sidney was a certified genius who had been hiding in stupid clothing for some obscure purpose too deep for mere mortals to understand. His high school teachers were embarrassed they had not discovered the ploy during so many years of having Sidney in their classes, but they figured if a real genius wanted to remain in high school half a dozen years or so, they should not be expected to know the reasons such a deep thinker might have ... perhaps he had planned to wait for his acne to clear.

Sidney advanced through his college curriculum until he was awarded a full scholarship, a Ph.D. and a Phi Beta Kappa key. He published profusely in the most obscure journals, got a hefty government grant in his specialty area of arthropod biology and delivered brilliant lectures to gaggles of students who drove to him in flocks (or vice versa). Sophie, who did all the work, chose to remain the unsung heroine, content to share silently in Sidney's blooming academic career.

But several years later Dr. Lemley was browsing through some old editions of the *Western Journal of Literature*. As luck would have it, he happened upon the treatise, written by another, a certain Sophocles Aphidoidea, which had sparked Sidney's undeserved success.

Indignant at this outrageous act of plagiarism, the professor took his find to the president of the university. However, by this time Sidney was president of the university and, with Sophie still in his ear, would hear none of it.

§

Fable 9 – Dreams

Bathed in sweat, heart pounding furiously, you wake up screaming something like, "Oh, please, Dr. Grimspar, can I take a makeup!" And then you realize that, of course, no one would be irresponsible enough to sleep through the alarm clock and miss a final exam.

The "missed final" dream is the brass ring of college nightmares, and though you may not have that particular one, you will have recurring nocturnal unpleasantries about your college classes until … well, I'll let you know when they stop.

How about the one dealing with the monster section of World History 101? There are 450 students packed into a lecture hall. Those in the back wear binoculars to see the board. In the dream, you rush in and, to your great surprise, it's test day on the five assigned chapters of the Roman conquests. You've read right up to the fall of Greece, the chapter preceding these five.

Multiple choice test forms are passed to the rear of the room. Proctors in white togas holding cats-o-nine-tails line the wall and they're shouting "pull, pull" as someone at the front of the room pounds a kettledrum. Your test form arrives and you open it to find triangles with lettered lines and angles. It's a trigonometry test after all, but you only had business math. You look at the paper of the girl next to you, and it's got triangles too, but she's breezing through it as though nothing's wrong. A proctor sees you peek and begins to shove students aside as he walks toward your desk with his whip whirling ….

Don't be alarmed. You knew it was a dream when the proctor resembled Russell Crowe. How about this one:

It's Introduction to Sociology 207 and this time the lecture hall only holds 200 students. You arrive for the midterm. Your professor, Dr. Glenda Wiltweed, passes out the exams and sits behind her desk on a riser at the front of the room. Then, delighting all, she picks up her papers and leaves the room. Within seconds, every student in the class whips out the

Proctors in white togas holding cats-o-nine-tails
line the wall and they're shouting "pull, pull" as someone
at the front of the room pounds a kettledrum.

textbook and boldly looks up the answers. You are faced with an impossible moral dilemma because you left your textbook at the dorm. Worse yet, the notes you did bring are no good because you missed the last six lectures.

What can you do? It's evident everyone in the class will make an "A" on the exam and your only hope for a "C" has just gone down the curved tube. The situation demands desperate measures. So you stand up and begin aloud, "Now classmates, let's just put our books away and take this test honestly." No one even looks up. You try again, and this time a finger taps your shoulder from behind. It's Dr. Wiltweed who demands to look at your notes. While the cheating continues all over the room, Dr. Wiltweed goes through your notebook and mutters things like, "Just as I suspected" and "What a disgrace!" You can't tell if she's talking about your notes or the fact that you wore only your pajamas to class.

In fairness, it should be pointed out that teachers have the same kinds of college nightmares. I'll share the one I have before the start of every semester:

Although I neglected to prepare for class, I'm going over some lecture notes from last semester I think will get me through. The bell rings, and I dash to the largest lecture hall in the building. Outside the door, a faculty colleague says my course in mass media didn't make this semester, so I have to teach this chemistry class, and go right in because I'm late.

Every chair is filled with eager students, all dressed in white lab coats and protective plastic face masks. It's a senior-level chemistry class, and the last time I failed chemistry was the first time I took it in high school. I haven't the slightest idea what I'm going to say, but it doesn't matter because when I begin speaking I have laryngitis and I can only croak a little bit. The students can't hear me, and I can see they're becoming agitated, so I start to tap dance. Several front rows of students file out of the room. Those students who remain are bemused by the dancing, but they begin to keep time by striking their pencils on the edge of their desks, and through the syncopation I notice four older men dressed in business suits in the back row.

The four men stand, and I see it's two full-professors, my dean and the president of the university. The dean shouts, "I heard you were weird, but this is one hell of a way for you to behave on your tenure evaluation!"

§

Fable 10 – 3.0 Grading

When a truly momentous academic change is introduced, this writer owes it to his audience to share the development.

Dr. Sayman R. Ukidin, deputy secretary of Higher Education Administration in the U.S. Department of Education, announced that the nation's accredited colleges and universities will begin reporting grades on a 3.0 system next fall. Ukidin said the move follows years of debate about lack of standardized grading. Two-thirds of America's higher education institutions report grades on a 4.0 system while the remaining one-third report on a 3.0 system.

"The difference has been a source of great concern by this country's employers who often have difficulty determining if their applicants graduated with an 'A-minus' or a 'C-plus' average," Ukidin said.

"Additionally, most of the prestigious private schools use the 3.0 system and sneer at the 4.0 grades awarded primarily by public universities," he disclosed. "Graduate school admission committees view a reported 3.7 GPA as grade inflation and dock the applicant accordingly. 'Why should we cheapen our standards to recognize a D and give it a point' the committees ask; 'a D is not even an average grade.'"

Finally, he noted, because the 3.0 system is based on an odd number instead of the even 4.0 number, there will be fewer ties in class rankings.

Ukidin said, "Those affected should not be overly concerned as the change will result in higher grades for most students. "It works like the present system with quality points and credits except .5 becomes the lowest 'D'; 1.25 the lowest 'C'; 2.0 the lowest 'B'; and 2.75 the lowest 'A' grade. Going from a 4.0 to a 3.0 system is pretty obvious," he said with a snide smirk. "Just multiply your present GPA by 75 percent. It's not rocket science."

He pointed to the "C-plus" student. "This student has a 2.75

Going from a 4.0 to a 3.0 system, is pretty obvious," Dr. Ukidin said with a smirk. "Just multiply your present GPA by 75 percent. It's not rocket science."

on the standard 4.0 system. The same student now earns a 2.06 on the 3.0 system, a 'B-minus' grade."

Asked about this wrinkle, Dr. Ukidin replied, "These students probably only miss a 'B' by a few fractional points anyway. Why penalize them for the likely consequences of a wild frat party in their freshman year? We can't all be saints, so why not just give it to them?"

The "D" and "F" students also will improve almost a letter grade. A former "D" average of 1.75 will move to 1.3, a low "C" grade, and the former "F" average of say .85 will become .64 on the 3.0 scale, a low but passable "D" grade equivalent.

Explaining the increase, Ukidin said, "We took this opportunity to make the road of the 'D' or 'F' student less rocky. Some of these students faced a nearly impossible task just to remain in school. Now they have only to raise their grades a little bit to show some evidence of trying, and they'll have their 'C' average soon enough."

He bristled at the suggestion that dorm vacancy rates or tuition revenue was associated with any part of the grade change decision.

Under the new system, a "B-plus" student will have only a mid-range "B" as their 3.3 average drops to 2.5.

Ukidin said he didn't think the difference at all critical.

"Anyone who would quibble about losing those paltry few tenths of a point can just go ahead and gripe. They still have a nice 'B' and should be quite satisfied."

Some noticeable GPA slippage does occur for a few students during the grade conversion. For example, an "A" student with a current 3.6 average will have a 2.7 in the new grading, a high "B-plus" grade.

"We argued long and hard about that one," Ukidin said. "If we worked it any other way, the new plan would become confusing. We believe a real academic achiever will not be at a disadvantage. Such students will easily be able to pull their grades up with a little extra effort and regain their former 'A' under the new system."

However, the Higher Education Committee recognized there

will be many fewer magna, summa or cum laude graduates.

"That would be a disaster," Ukidin said. "It would ruin the pomp and circumstance of the graduation exercise and would not provide parents or professors the proper recognition they deserve on their special day, although everyone would get home earlier."

In its wisdom, the committee resolved the dilemma equitably.

"A note signed by a recognized academic administrator on official university letterhead will be attached to these students' permanent transcript indicating their average is actually somewhat higher than it might appear," Dr. Ukidin said, "like the warning on a car's rearview mirror."

§

Fable 11 – Tricks

Limited resources – time or money – often result in the adoption of expedient procedures. For instance, it is rumored that Kansas (or perhaps Nebraska or Colorado … it's hard to tell from the highway) wanted to show it enforced the national Interstate speed limit to qualify for federal funding. Lacking funds to hire sufficient state troopers, the law enforcement agencies decided simply to put up signs reading "Warning: Radar Patrolled Speed Limit" and "Speed Checked by Airplane."

While their harmless ploy certainly raises ethical questions by deceiving motorists, this subterfuge slowed would-be speeders, and in such a case the means probably justifies the end.

Those in higher education, under the pressures of time and tenure requirements, occasionally resort to the same kinds of little tricks for expediency's sake or perhaps just self-preservation. I'll tell one on myself.

It was the large lecture section of a freshman-level survey of something-or-other class with limited seating in the room. In fact, students packed the place shoulder-to-shoulder, which might be fine for sharing body warmth in the winter and for budding romances, but it caused problems at test time.

Some young faculty members believe they should contribute to a student's educational experience by giving short-essay exams. While this has benefits – it is more difficult to copy neighbors' essay answers – one weekend experience of grading 150 essay exams convinces the neophyte faculty member that multiple-choice exams are by far the superior testing procedure. The disadvantage is that test answers are easily copied, particularly so if students are packed into a room eyeball-to-eyeball. What is one to do?

One could devise three different forms of the test and distribute them so no two students sitting together would have the same form. But that takes time, extra copying work and,

One weekend experience of grading 150 essay exams convinces the neophyte faculty member that multiple-choice exams are by far the superior testing procedure.

yes, extra thinking. I confess to having used the same test form but changing the color of the paper on the top test sheet. "Now you people with the green form," I'd say, "make sure you have all 12 pages of the exam."

Of course, I still have occasional pangs of conscience about this prank, but that's nothing compared with the guilt Dr. Gertrude Ganglia of the political science department must have felt.

Dr. Gerty was an old-timer who knew the ins and outs of university life. She opted for the easy outs whenever she could. It was Ganglia who ripped one of those large metal signs from the bowels of the library: "WARNING: This is Not an Exit. Alarm Will Sound If Opened," and she hammered it to the outside of her faculty office door. Students thought the door was a fire escape. Dr. Gerty could get her work done without interruption, but since students never knocked, she didn't bother keeping office hours.

It was Ganglia who put a message on her answering machine at home: "I am eager to speak with you, but a minor medical emergency prevents my coming to the phone at this time. I may be late for class tomorrow."

Dr. Ganglia knew all the angles. When asked to serve on committees, she welcomed the offer. At the meetings, she disagreed with the majority on every issue and was most vocal when decisions approached unanimity. Her committee members were greatly relieved when she stopped attending. They said nothing about her absence and kept her name on the membership roster.

She was the one who dropped nickels instead of quarters in the faculty coffee club piggy bank, and though everyone knew she did it, no one dared confront her.

But the cruelest tricks of all were those Dr. Ganglia played on her classes:
- Her lectures were fascinating and riddled with bawdy tidbits about historic political figures until just past the drop date, and then she read aloud from the textbook;
- She graded student papers on a five-point scale instead

of giving letter grades because she knew she'd get fewer complaints when she gave a student a 2.25 instead of a "D";

• She told her weakest students not to worry, they could try harder and pull up their grades before the end of the semester;

• She allowed students to drop their lowest test grade so she wouldn't have to give make-up exams. "That's okay," she would say, "If you can't be here, we just won't count the zero you would have gotten. Of course, you'll have to keep that last low mark you received";

• She assigned term papers and then graded them solely on the number of footnotes;

• She formed student "teams" for oral presentations under the guise that stronger students can help the weaker students along. Then she had team members grade one another anonymously, knowing that the weakest students would always get the lowest average anyway, and the strongest students would get blasted by one or two of the weaker students just out of spite;

• She sympathetically offered extra credit assignments for students who had less than a "C" grade at midterm knowing full well those students would never do additional work. "Gosh," she would say later, "I sure hoped you'd take advantage of those extra credit opportunities."

• She feigned generosity by telling students she would drop the five lowest assignment grades they got and count only their 10 best grades. But she knew only the "A" students would ever do more than the minimum 10 assignments, so all the rest would be stuck with the grades she gave them on those. If a student complained about getting a bad grade on a paper she'd say, "Don't worry, you can always drop that one";

• She took off for spelling!

I don't know what became of Dr. Ganglia. She left our school and was rumored to be making big bucks in campaign consulting. If you run into her, tell her I asked, "How's tricks?"

§

Fable 12 – Learning Center

If large ships can have little dinghies, why shouldn't universities have learning centers? Yes, a special Learning Center at a university does sound redundant, and it probably confuses parents of incoming freshmen on orientation day when the guide says: "Now here's the University and over here is the Learning Center." Parents embarrass themselves by asking if any learning took place in universities before there were Learning Centers.

Actually, Learning Centers developed the same way many other fine institutions came about: because of euphemistic indexing. Try finding a gas station in a telephone directory; are they listed under filling stations or service stations? Teachers who called Supplies Inventory for a box of chalk were told no, that's in the bookstore. Students who called the bookstore for test scanning forms were told no, those are in the Computer Center. Projectors are at the Media Center, but film is at Supplies Inventory while cameras are in the academic departments, but no, they don't loan them. Math tutorials are available in the Remedial Studies Center and foreign language lab CDs are in the library ... and these are just the telephone indexing mistakes about equipment. Locating people and services got even worse. So schools tried to centralize their ancillary supplies in Learning Centers but, as frequently happens in bureaucratic institutions, things got out of hand.

Dr. Harvey Lugwinder, a freshly minted Ed.D. and assistant professor of education, was put in charge of the Learning Center at a small state college in the Rocky Mountain area. His days were pleasant because the Learning Center consisted of only his small office and a closet, no other staff and a single overhead projector (it was kept in the closet). One day the president called and asked Lugwinder to prepare a three-minute slide show titled "An Extended Tour of Our Library."

Lugwinder told him it was impossible. The Learning Center

Schools tried to centralize their ancillary supplies in Learning Centers, but, as frequently happens in bureaucratic institutions, things got out of hand.

had no equipment, no staff and no budget. The president would not be dissuaded. "Lugwinder," he replied menacingly, "the only department that has any of that stuff is Men's Athletics. Get me that slide show or you're the new rifle team coach."

"Big deal," Lugwinder thought, but inquiries revealed the last three rifle team coaches had previously headed the Learning Center, and none had survived the demotion. In a panic, he did what many other freshly minted doctorates do: He wrote a grant proposal.

Governments have an old adage about college funding: "Tuition, no way; Bricks, okay." It means statehouses look askance at college giveaways such as student loans, but they will support higher education by helping erect massive buildings and providing the necessary equipment to fill them.

When the federal government agency's committee read Lugwinder's grant proposal, they laughed out loud. "Here's a guy at a state school where there isn't another university for 500 miles, probably near a bona fide Native American reservation, and he asks for $2,000 to do a slide show. It must be some kind of joke. We'll just add a few zeros." By unanimous approval, the committee awarded Lugwinder $2 million in equipment and another half million in supplies over a three-year period.

The stuff began arriving by truck and train. Lugwinder called the federal agency and said he had no place to put it and no one to operate it. "No problem," the committee said.

In a short time the Learning Center grew into a sprawling, carnivorous, totally self-sustaining entity. Lugwinder used the equipment and funding as carrots to ingratiate himself to chairpersons all over campus, and these departments begged to affiliate with the Learning Center and share in its bounty. Lugwinder took in the practical departments – those whose graduates could command high paying jobs – but he left all the loose baggage (history, philosophy, art, etc.) behind.

The Learning Center, now called The Center of Higher Learning, developed its own curriculum, offered remedial courses and university credit classes, had its own satellite television production facilities, held international workshops and seminars, became accredited, and began to consider adding an intercollegiate sports program.

So well had Lugwinder administered his Learning Center that it now dwarfed the former university proper. It had more enrollment, more programs and more graduates. In fact, when The Center of Higher Learning needed more room to expand, Lugwinder bought the old campus and closed the former university. It was all duplication anyway, and not very good duplication at that.

He did keep one activity and one hold-out from the old campus: the former president, who is now dodging rounds at the old rifle range.

§

Fable 13 – Logic I

I can remember the days when logic classes were a means to an end. They existed for those too stupid to pass the minimum mathematics requirement, Math 101.

We freshmen came in droves, smiling foolishly like a herd of cattle that had thought the man said "fodder" house instead of "slaughter" house.

I will never forget that first day in Logic I. I hadn't bothered to bring pencil or paper. My mind was on the pool game I would begin as soon as the bell rang. Jocks ambled and golden-curled coeds skipped lightly to their chairs, and most went immediately to sleep.

When the opening bell rang, the door slammed shut, revealing the professor who had been hiding behind it since the night before. He leaped to the lock and bolted it. Everyone gasped as he took the key, swallowed it and turned to glare at the class. It was Dr. Xenious, the infamous "Dr. X," protector of no one, flunker of legions. He chortled, baring hideously sharp, plaque-laced fangs.

Fear hung over the room like a nasty black cloud. Only the audible stiffening of joints broke the silence as adrenalin rushed through pulsing veins. A cold shiver of fright made its way down my spine as I sensed I should have taken Math 101, knowing for certain I would never have passed it.

Dr. Xenious made his way to the front of the room. He paused before the frailest looking girl on the front row who stared up at him in wide-eyed wonder. He leaned in close to her face and shouted, "What is logic?" Her chair tipped over backward sprawling her to the floor. She spent the rest of the class period ripping green tiles from the linoleum with her fingernails and stacking them neatly in her lap. I cannot say if she dropped out of school, but she certainly wasn't in class the next day.

Matter of fact, pitifully few of us showed up to class that next day, but our mass exodus did not seem to satisfy Dr. Xenious.

Dr. Xenious paused before the frailest looking girl, leaned in close and shouted, "What is logic?"

He began a second lecture.

He had a thick accent derived from his Greek origin. He told us that two very important words in logic embodied the heart of the discipline. These, he explained, were "relevant" and "irrelevant." But his accent sounded particularly heavy at the beginning of the two words: He trilled his R's so dramatically that both words came out "rrrelevant." So there was rrrelevant and rrrelevant. If he deemed something rrrelevant, we were to write it down and memorize it for the next test. Conversely, if he deemed something rrrelevant, we were to ignore it as an illogical figment of philosophical gobbledygook. While the rule was difficult for me to understand, I figured it was probably rrrelevant anyway so I chalked it off and wrote it down for the next exam.

Dr. Xenious was above the class. He was logical. Frequently, he posed questions for the class to discuss. One example was the following: "If a man is righteous, just, and in a position to offer life-and-death decisions, and if this man allows a prisoner to choose his own punishment, how much is a bowl of chili in a diner by the railroad track and why – be specific."

The remaining jock, who was frantically taking notes, thinks he knows, so he offers an explanation which is clearly rrrelevant to the question. Dr. Xenious is appalled. He knows the explanation is rrrelevant but instead of turning to someone else he turns on the jock. "That is rrridiculous. You should be ashamed to open your mouth. You should be ashamed to breathe, you rrretched jelly-headed ignoramus!" or words to that effect.

I found out why the university accepts logic as a substitute for freshman math. One day on the way to the pool hall, I dropped my logic book. It fell open two-thirds of the way through, far past the point I had ever looked in any of my freshman textbooks. And there, staring back at me, were what looked like algebraic equations. In a philosophy book! I tried out one of the problems which, to the best of my recollection, went something like: "All men are mortal. Socrates is a man. Therefore Socrates is a mortician." This is called a syllogism, and they got trickier by the page. The chapters that followed were written in equations with no text at all. The only thing to do was to stall the class to keep Dr. X from getting to those chapters. I tried.

"Dr. Xenious, when I was reading the assigned chapter, I was stumped by the proposition that virtue is its own reward. Could you expound on that for today's class?"

"Cretin!" he shouted. "Rrreprobate! Rrrapscallion! You are so rrresponsible (I knew he meant irresponsible) that you haven't rrread a single chapter this entire term. Every semester some rrrascal tries to keep the class from getting to the math section, and I had eight-to-five you would be the imbecilic rrretch who tries to fool a logic professor."

When the semester was over, the jock got a "B-minus" and I flunked. But it was fair because the jock actually studied. I now had a required credit to make up and no intention of repeating Logic I or taking Math 101. Luckily, I had eked by in other classes that first semester and was no longer part of the freshman herd, easily influenced by advisers needing to fill classes. I waited until I was a junior and took a qualifying philosophy class in marriage and family relations. It was rrrelevant, too, but I got my "C-plus" and thereby fulfilled my college math requirement.

§

Fable 14 – Counselors

I would be the last to say a guidance counselor has no purpose. In fact, I have a set of bookends in the caricature of guidance counselors who sit with pained expressions and stare quite intently, each at a different wall of my study.

I have a theory about counselors who help students through college. It is simply: The number of years a student spends in college is proportional to the number of times that student visits a counselor.

At small private schools where tuition is high, counselors are well paid for their ability to keep a student happy. Students entering the counselor's office will be greeted by a warm smile and friendly handshake. The student lies prone on a plush, leather couch and airs his troubles. The counselor takes notes, asks questions about the student's childhood and feelings toward his mother. When the session concludes, the counselor walks the student to the door, wishes him luck in all his endeavors, then returns to the office to shred the notes and resume slumber on the plush leather couch.

But the sprawling public campuses rarely feature this pleasant interlude. At today's mega-universities, counselors are hindered by the scant minutes they can spend with each student. The case of John Philip Sousa Jones represents an all-too-common one.

A born musician, Jones played in the New York Philharmonic at age 7, took private lessons his entire life and decided to go to college to get his music doctorate. With hope in his heart and his shiny, brass sousaphone draped around his neck, Jones entered the registration line and met his guidance counselor.

Mr. Grizzley Hardtack, in charge of guidance for H through L, had spoken to nearly 200 students in the last hour. He saw Jones coming and sized the lad up as he approached the table.

Hardtack used his own pet formula, devised after his first day as a rookie guidance counselor. He noticed Jones had brown

With hope in his heart, Jones entered the registration line and met his guidance counselor.

eyes and black hair, an easy student to classify. The lad stood before him now, and Hardtack wasted no time.

"J.P.S. Jones. Ah, Jones, I see you have three initials before your surname. That's kind of unusual. Probably named after a couple of uncles to please your mother's side, eh? Well, it happens all the time ... nothing to be ashamed of.

"No, don't tell me, let me guess. You're interested in building: design, structure, physics. That's good, Jones. I can always spot an engineer. So disciplined, so introspective.

"Well, Jones, we have just the place for you, and I know you're going to do well in all your expectations. Take this green slip, go to the table on your left and report to the engineering building Monday. Next!"

Monday found Jones in Physics 101, seated between Daniel Jones, with black hair and brown eyes, and Melinda Jones, also with black hair and brown eyes.

When the professor, Dr. Luther Jones, called the roll, an even stranger coincidence became evident. Every student in the room was a Jones, except Bill Kowens and Gwendolyn Holmes.

By the end of the semester, most of the class including John Philip had flunked. Dr. Luther Jones, who seemed to know little more than his students, apologized and confessed his secret desire to be a dermatologist.

John Philip reported to his counselor immediately after receiving the "F." He was a bit perturbed about his lost semester and eager to get back to his double bass.

Hardtack had been through a difficult morning. He had already signed off on perhaps 50 forged medical excuses for cut classes and was in no mood to trifle. John Philip entered the office and slammed the door behind him. "Mr. Hardtack," he began, but was promptly cut off there by his counselor.

"Well, John, that was quite a forceful entrance. I admire a lad with gumption. And that voice ... so deep ... so resonant. Why I bet you have powerful lungs and larynx, and just look at those bulging cheeks, amazing! Public speaking, that's the ticket; you're a natural politician. Here, take this blue card and report to speech communication Monday. Good day, senator."

Monday found Jones in Communication 101 with all the other Joneses who had been his classmates in physics. And the professor, Howard William Jones, had the same deer-caught-in-the-headlights expression as Dr. Luther. Another semester down the drain.

After several more brief encounters with his counselor, Jones went into pharmacy, then switched to philosophy, biology and journalism.

Mr. Hardtack had long grown weary of watching the same faces pass catatonically through the same old routine. He once asked himself, "Why can't these darn kids ever stick with something?" But even in his exasperation the counselor was not dismayed. If all else failed, there was always elementary education, where they could pass on their accumulated knowledge to the next generation.

§

Fable 15 – Grad Teaching Assistants

Have pity on the poor graduate teaching assistant and, occasionally, on the poor undergraduate who has the poor graduate teaching assistant as an instructor.

Universities have taken a haughty position recently on graduate teaching assistants. Some schools have gone so far as to demand graduate assistants be certified in their ability to speak English before being approved as classroom instructors. The purpose is less an attempt to eliminate foreign language speakers but designed more to prevent course instruction by mumblers, whisperers, chokers, droners, snorers and whistlers. Possessing understandable speaking skills is a rather harsh prerequisite for university teaching, and thankfully, one that hasn't been extended to the full-time faculty.

But with the recent reliance on low-paid graduate assistants as classroom teachers, I am reminded of my own nemesis, Mr. Mitchell Efflefoos, or as students in our class affectionately called him, Mitch the Match.

I remember nothing about the subject matter of English 101, but I'll never forget The Match. It was his first teaching experience, and he was absolutely petrified of his students because he had never spoken publicly before an audience larger than his bathroom mirror. He was the kind of teacher who, in an effort to seem relaxed and natural, would walk in front of his desk and sit on the edge of it, but would invariably slide off and barely maintain balance enough to miss the two students in the front row (the front row remained empty after the first class meeting).

Now, this was back in the days when college teachers smoked in class: Who could deny a professor his pipe? The Match was a smoker, and under the extreme tension of having to lecture, a chain smoker. He took cigarettes from one of the two packs in his

Mitch the Match was a smoker, and under
the extreme tension of having to lecture, a chain smoker.

shirt pocket and rolled them between his fingers, occasionally pointing them for emphasis as he lectured. Frequently he broke them while he was talking and had to brush tobacco off the front of his jacket. He put them to his lips, but his lips were so dry the cigarettes often fell to the floor. And through it all he continued to lecture as if unaware of this awkward ritual. When he successfully placed one, he lectured through clenched lips while the cigarette dangled and bobbed. And then the real show began.

He reached for his little box of Red Diamond matches. Apparently he had cornered the market on them because he had them in every pocket, and he needed all his matches to get through a class period. Eyes remained riveted on his every motion as the matches were taken from the box and struck against the flint-like compound on its side.

A nervous smoker goes through a mountain of matches, and Mitchell personified nervousness. He'd strike and miss, strike and break, and strike again. When he finally did actually light one, there was no guarantee it would be the winning match as Mitchell's vacillating breath usually blew it out before he could light the cigarette. The only time he paused in the lecture was when he had to inhale to finally light the cigarette. He'd beam with accomplishment and continue to lecture as he tried to shake out the match, the climax of the show. He attempted this with wide waves of his arm and hand, but the match almost never went out on the first try, or the fourth. Mitchell's eyes would fill with tears as the still-lighted matches scorched his fingers. And even as the smell of smoldering flesh filled the room and the corners of his mouth winced in pain, he was never daunted: The lecture went on without interruption.

When the match did go out, Mitchell would toss it at the wastebasket by the door, some 10 feet away. Thankfully, he never tossed a lighted match, but when the students witnessed this three-point basket attempt the first day, they all sat away from the door in case he erred and set the wastebasket on fire. Through the entire semester, he never once landed a match in the basket, although he rimmed it twice. I lost a lot of lunch money betting on him.

In truth, it is unfair to claim that I never learned anything about English from Mitch the Match. I have only reviewed the highlights of that semester. There's a lot to be learned in English 101, even if the semester is spent huddled elbow-to-elbow with other students in the back four rows in one corner of the room. I did learn something, and you may, too, from the next exciting episode of the continuing saga of graduate teaching assistants.

§

Fable 16 – Grad TAs, the sequel

When we left my freshman English teacher, a graduate assistant who tried to hide his fear of classroom lecturing behind a cloud of cigarette smoke, the students huddled into one corner of the room, both to avoid having Mitchell Efflefoos land in their laps and to avoid being too close to the wastebasket when he set it afire with his matches.

Mitch the Match (or Smoky the Bore, as we sometimes called him), had succeeded in one pedagogical goal. He had managed to keep everyone's attention riveted on the lecturer. But his students' main concerns were their fascination with his cigarette lighting and, of course, self-preservation, not the subject matter. Still, I must confess I learned something about English 101. For example, there was the whole issue of commas.

As strange as it may seem, Mitchell was doing his doctoral dissertation on commas. He had spent the past two years eating, sleeping and smoking the little devils, and his extensive research convinced him that the best of them was no damn good. The Match didn't begin the semester by saying, "I'm doing my dissertation on commas," because his students were only freshmen and might have mistakenly inferred a hierarchy by which English departments award dissertation topics. They might have believed Mitchell didn't rate a Shakespeare topic or even a "Young Goodman Brown" but had been relegated to commas as some sort of punishment – perhaps he had singed the garment of one of his major professors. So Mitchell revealed nothing but lurked in the shadows waiting for our first theme assignments to be turned in.

I had used 27 commas in a two-page theme. Twenty-four had been circled in red and these, plus the eight misspellings, resulted in an "F." Several other students suffered a similar fate.

My next theme had only 12 commas and on the returned paper 10 had been circled in red and these, plus the five misspellings, resulted in a "D." It was beginning to look bad for me because a grade of less than a "B" in English 101 meant having to pass the senior English Proficiency Exam. While I believe a comma should be used where it is required, according to the rules of proper grammar, I must admit having compromised my principles on that third theme. I wrote three pages and used only three commas. Upon return, two were circled in red and these, plus the four misspellings resulted in a "C." I was learning something in English 101.

Paragraphs ... not much to 'em really. You have something to say and you say it, then move on. You don't write about your kid sister's dolls and mix them up with drag car racing. You start a new paragraph. It's that simple, or so I thought.

But no, Mitch informed us. You begin with a topic sentence that outlines your theme for that paragraph and states the several points you intend to make. Then you actually make the points in the order you outlined at the beginning and put a summary sentence at the end. Only then should you go on to the next paragraph where you repeat the process. Such a complex paragraph could continue for a full page, so there might be only one or two paragraphs in a three-page paper. Apparently, Mitch believed that paragraphs were just bloated commas: the fewer the better. Everything about this process offended my sense of writing decorum but, I must confess, I acquiesced to get my "B."

Another incident I will never forget was part of the between-cigarette lecture portions in which Mitch the Match told the class, with a straight face, that the novel *The Adventures of Tom Sawyer* was an allegory. Every time Huckleberry Finn crossed the Mississippi on his raft from town to the island, he went from good to evil, from civilization to the primeval, from responsibility to undisciplined debauchery. And what is more, our graduate teaching assistant told us, Mark Twain intended this exact moral lesson when he wrote the book!

I could just see that rascal Samuel Clemens, that sly old fox, at his writing table. "Now, let's see," he'd say, scratching his white mane with the point of his quill pen, "where did I leave

I could just see that rascal Samuel Clemens, that sly old fox, at his writing table. "Now, let's see," he'd say.

ol' Huck Finn? Was he on the good side of the river or was he on the evil side? Will my readers get the full import of this novel? Will they understand how painstakingly I've developed the allegory of crossing the Mississippi River? Will graduate teaching assistants ever share the finding with their freshman English classes? Has my life's work been an utter waste on those poor clods who only read my writing for enjoyment?"

I simply could not restrain myself. For the first time that semester, I spoke in class.

"Mr. Efflefoos," I said, "meaning no disrespect sir, but Twain's writings fill an entire library shelf, and nobody sees allegories in his other works. I just find it hard to believe he wrote *Tom Sawyer* for any other purpose than to tell a good story."

"Stone, isn't it?" Efflefoos intoned. "Are you aware that making less than a 'B' in this class requires you to take the senior English Proficiency Exam?"

I don't remember anything else about English 101, but I do remember the senior English Proficiency Exam. I used commas where they are required according to the standard rules of grammar, broke my paragraphs into edible portions and I passed, although I did rather poorly on the spelling section.

§

Fable 17 – Insecure

Faculty members may seem the epitome of self-confidence. However, that air of wisdom, of control and worldliness, is often learned on the job. Like a medical doctor, judge or banker, the professor finds he or she has grown into playing an expected role and then forgets the time when those lines had to be memorized. The only thing worse for a faculty member than becoming a pompous prima donna is failure to adopt the lofty airs students and colleagues expect. Such a professor becomes not just a misfit but riddled with self-doubt, and insecurity was the middle name of Dr. Susan I. Swizzlestix.

That wasn't her real name, of course, but this story is so sad and of such a sensitive nature that the fear of lawsuits requires a nom de guerre. She used to be just Susie Swizzlestix, a quiet child whose parents expected too much of her. And as an only child, she was forced to give it to them. She had always thought of herself as just a diligent overachiever. She studied hard for every quiz in school and shared her doubts with both friends, who grew sick of listening. You know the fretful type:

"I'm so scared," Susie would tell them. "I just didn't study enough, and I know I'm going to fail this quiz."

"Oh, gag me with a steam shovel," her friends would say. "You're going to make a 98 and set the curve for the entire class."

And it happened every time. Through assiduously hard work she had become an honor student, but her candid insecurity left her friendless. She pondered upon this. "If I'm so smart, why didn't I know to keep my mouth shut? So I must not be smart; it must only be the hard work. And why can I only make 98s instead of 100s?" Those paradoxes plagued her through adolescence and even through her years at Vassar where she was graduated magna cum laude.

She went on to Berkeley Graduate School and earned two master's degrees, then earned a law degree at Columbia and

Susie went on to Berkeley Graduate School and earned two master's degrees, then earned a law degree at Columbia and completed her doctorate at Emory on full scholarship.

completed her doctorate at Emory on full scholarship. But through it all she questioned whether she was worthy of a career in higher education. So many of her fellow students seemed more creative, more brilliant than she. Hers were just the fruits of dogged hard work and a little luck, she thought.

When she became Dr. Susan Swizzlestix, she got an assistant professorship at a prestigious university. One might think that would be the end of it: She would wrap herself in the mantle of dignified glory that comes with the teaching turf; no one would ever question her worth or abilities, and of course that would have been the case, except for her own insecurity. But self-doubt is insidious. Even as the years passed, she wondered if she were really faculty material or just a sham in velvet cloak.

In her own excessively organized way, she created a list entitled, "Am I like other faculty?" She formed two columns, the first headed, "YES," and it read like this:

1) My handwriting is illegible;
2) I can't carry a tune;
3) I tell students the first day of class I hope they all get "As," then I grade on a strict curve;
4) I can't remember students' names;
5) I forget to turn in my grades;
6) I have only three outfits I wear to class every week;
7) I can never balance my checkbook.

The second column, headed "NO," contained self-traits she recognized were different from her faculty colleagues:

1) I never park illegally on campus;
2) When students ask me a question and I don't know, I tell them I don't know;
3) I don't like coffee;
4) I really do enjoy advising students who haven't the slightest idea what they want out of college and probably shouldn't be here in the first place;
5) I get along with my dean;
6) I look forward to working on my class preparations, doing my grading and serving on committees.

She looked at the list and noted she was more like other

faculty than different. She recognized, as well, that there were other "faculty traits" she shared with colleagues. For example, she talked to herself aloud and had begun muttering replies. Every day when she left her office, she walked about half a mile to the spot she had parked her car the day before and then had to walk back to where she left it that day.

Even with the passing of her tenure year, Dr. Swizzlestix remained insecure about her place on faculty. She knew colleagues who had published books, written dozens of journal articles, gotten research grants, developed formulas and held patents that had made them rich. Some even did workshops at airport hotels where attendees paid $500 registration fees. They were brilliant; they belonged. While she had written two books and published a string of journal articles and had gotten a couple of middling grants, she didn't think these accomplishments stacked up, and they had taken countless hours of debilitating hard work.

Dr. Swizzlestix's insecurity had brought her close to a breakdown. In her desperation to resolve the dilemma, she visited the head of the school's Human Resources office, a former industrial psychologist, and revealed all. She hoped to take one of those vocational aptitude tests (the kind where if you already know what you want to be, you just answer the questions that way and it confirms your aspirations).

But Mr. Cogburn said the test was completely unnecessary. "You've given me enough information to write an insipid novel," he said, "and this list you showed me confirms my suspicions. Dr. Swizzlestix, you are both like other faculty members and unlike them. The solution is clear. You must become a department chairperson!"

Later that year, Dr. Swizzlestix was promoted to department head, and self-doubt never again troubled her. She had neither the time nor the resources.

§

Fable 18 – Evaluations

The teacher evaluation process is sweeping the nation. Universities are eager to rate teachers to make them more concerned with their classroom teaching rather than their research, grants and evening moonlighting with spatula at the local burger joint.

The high-status schools have been among the leaders in developing faculty evaluation forms but have not been foolish enough to use them on their own campuses. Instead, they exported the forms to lesser-status schools, which adopted them with fervor because they like to think of themselves as teaching-first institutions since they certainly aren't research institutions, although they certainly would prefer to be.

While the high-status schools don't fool around with in-class faculty evaluations, these same schools have instead been the hotbed of those little student-produced "guides" to the college, its courses and its teachers. In fact, one can almost group schools according to quality based on whether there is an "insider's guide" published by students.

While such guides are noble endeavors, they destroy the mystery of college and decrease the excitement of meeting class for the first time. Why bother even going to class at all if the information is carried in the guide? Students deserve to find out about their classes the old-fashioned way: gossip in the halls and trial-and-error. Surely that's how life operates in the workaday world as well.

I'm also opposed to the guides because I've read a few, and I think composing one is far too much of a good time for the writers. Snide remarks are certain to find their way into the brief. For example:

PHOTOSYNTHESIS 203: Prof. Ernie Bottomphiefer. Though a boring course to begin with, "Old Lush" as students call him, livens up the hour a little. Clad in red sneakers that

A far superior system was created by Dr. Armstrong Sitzbath, whose theory revolutionized teacher evaluations.

match his nose, "Beetface" delivers a truly remarkable (often unintelligible) lecture. He is fond of quoting poetry at length.

EDUCATION 418: Dr. Sarah "Chalkie" Dentmore. Expect the usual monotone her students have heard for the last 35 years. Expect the same information, as well. Class topics include recommended steps in filling out lesson plans and innovative methods for cleaning erasers. Education majors don't count sheep at night, they count "Chalkies."

Now, whether your campus has the student-prepared guide or the formal in-class teacher evaluation instrument, we should recognize that conscientious professors – those who really want to know if they are reaching their students – have devised their own evaluations. Prof. Gilbert W. Nitpicker, a bright young sociology teacher, thought he might be demanding too much of his students. So to evaluate his methods, he announced on the last day of class that each student must turn in a 12-page typewritten opinion sheet, footnoted and with bibliography, of what they thought of him as a teacher. He promised to grade the reports fairly.

Nitpicker's students rose in a body and stormed the rostrum. They dragged their instructor out to the flagpole and hoisted him to half-staff. The professor was pleased his evaluation system had been so successful and vowed to make adjustments in his future teaching just before the rope broke.

Dr. Armstrong Sitzbath created a far superior system. It was his theory that revolutionized teacher evaluations. He believed a teacher could find out what his students thought of him by reading the doodles on their desks at the end of the semester.

Before the first day of class, the good doctor sanded each desktop smooth. He would grin with satisfaction as he watched the data mount. Hundreds of pens, pencils, crayons and pocketknives revealed the hidden opinions of his students.

At the end of the semester, imagine his astonishment when he approached the first desktop and found a perfect copy of the Mona Lisa done in rich oils. Not far from the artist's desk was that of a physics major. On this desk was scratched the technique for capturing geothermal energy, with a few corrections penciled in to improve the original design. And on the desk behind the energy procedure, another student had created the strategy that would have turned the Battle of Gettysburg into a Confederate victory.

Sitzbath was stunned as he gazed around the room. Political debates, a reproduction of the Magna Carta, chemical formulas, a list of the capitals and export commodities of South American countries, a trajectory for a rocket flight to Saturn, poetry, essays and short stories filled the desktops.

The professor felt his system had failed and resolved to give up the profession entirely. Then he thought of the "A-plus" student in his room, the only "A" grade in the class. The doctor wondered what was on her desk.

He walked to the back of the room, and there on her desk, in black pencil, was a stick-figure caricature of a man and under it the inscription, "Sitzbath sucks eggs."

§

Fable 19 – The Scholar

Every campus has one. A resident intellectual: The Scholar. Unfortunately, the only recognition The Scholar will receive is from his students and behind his back, of course. The Scholar is the only person on campus – or in the greater world – with an all-consuming concern for such lofty questions as how many angels can dance on the head of a pin. The Scholar doesn't give a hoot about the theological implications. He only wants to know the number, and believes he will find out through sufficient library research.

Some might say thank goodness there is only one Scholar per campus. With luck, if the school is large enough, the statistical odds of ever having The Scholar for a class instructor are minuscule. Taking The Scholar's class might mean dealing with those ethereal problems all semester. I know because I beat the odds.

He was Dr. Craigmont Luffenfluff, a white-haired gentleman of medium build who wore a different cravat every day but with similar coffee stains. He was my graduate school professor for Seminar in Theories of What (I don't remember). I had always thought "seminar" meant a discussion, but Dr. Luffenfluff's seminar was an endless soliloquy to a captured audience. We would raise our hands and wait to be recognized, but the professor knew none of us could lend anything of merit to the incredibly wide range of topics he had been studying for years. For instance:

1. Young male members of a species of monkey in a remote region of Africa have been known to crouch in the bushes at the side of the road when they hear a truck approaching. One young monkey sticks his posterior far enough into the path of the oncoming vehicle to do himself serious bodily injury if hit. However, at the last possible instant, the monkey leaps out of the way and saunters off into the jungle, to the wild approval of his onlooking group of young monkeys.

Scientific experimentation found that a honey bee's figure-eight dance pattern shows the direction of food from the hive, while speed of the tail wagging indicates distance.

Is it a male mating ritual? Is it a status prank similar to those teenage boys play? Is it a monkey's way of flirting with suicide? Dr. Luffenfluff hadn't yet determined.

2. Consider the wag-tail dance of the honey bee on the hive. This is a centuries-old mystery, but scientific experimentation discovered that the direction of the figure-eight dance pattern indicates the direction of food from the hive (in relation to the sun's rays, of course). And the speed of the tail wagging indicates how far away from the hive food can be found. Both portions of the dance directions take into account any obstacle between the hive and the food, and that's probably why bees aren't found pasted to the walls of buildings.

3. Why is the district pollsters use to help predict the outcome of an election called a bellwether district? It is because the oldest male sheep, or "wether," leads the flock. Since the other sheep follow the wether, the shepherd hangs a bell on the old fellow to find the flock in case they pull a Little Bo Peep. The pollsters' district is selected on the assumption other districts will follow its history of voting for the winning candidate.

These were just some of the snippets relating to animals. Dr. Luffenfluff offered equally enigmatic lectures on linguistics differentiating lexicography from symbology and phonetics, on math (which baffled me because I don't know what prime marks mean) and on 20th century international politics. Don't get the impression this was an early version of Trivial Pursuit because each lecture was very carefully documented with author, title and date, and because Dr. Luffenfluff did not merely present the dry facts, he grappled with their meaning.

The high point of the class happened when a fellow student, Monty Dryrott, tried to take on The Scholar. Monty was a pushy, unpleasant youth whose only redeeming quality (in this instance) was his knowledge of Communism. He claimed he was a Communist and quoted doctrine at great length, although he could be paid to shut up. Monty had prepared for the challenge and caught The Scholar on the last day of class, just as he was refuting a Stalin fallacy.

"Dr. Luffenfluff," Monty interrupted, "Elwood Smith's

book, *Stalin: Truth or Consequences*, clearly shows the instance you just mentioned was wrongly attributed to Stalin."

You could have heard a snowflake drop as The Scholar stared Monty down. We figured Luffenfluff had never before been spoken to by a student in class and was not taking it well. But after a few seconds The Scholar responded:

"Elwood Smith was a pseudonym. The Central Party commissioned that book to discredit Lenin. You will find an account in Robert Green's diary, *Kremlin Party Down* (1956, Putnum)," he said.

"But Green's diary was a forgery, as Walters proved in his thesis, (The Ohio State University, 1963)," Monty said heatedly.

"No, Green's second diary *Capers with Khrushchev* was the forgery as shown in Dameron's article 'Behind Closed Walls,' (Journal of International Intrigue, 1971)."

The argument continued for nearly 15 minutes with each of the combatants drawing on a wealth of references. I was most impressed when Dr. Luffenfluff mentioned a little-known text published by the Hungarian People's Press in 1932, and Monty retorted coldly that The Scholar was mistaken, but Dr. Luffenfluff said, "the spiral-bound edition available at the monastery on the Tibetan border." There was a long pause.

"Sir," Monty said, "I believe you are correct." He was badly shaken by the experience, but The Scholar calmly finished the lecture as if nothing out of the ordinary had occurred.

What was the good of the class? What does a real Scholar provide for humanity in the greater scheme of things? I'm not exactly sure, but then I'm not quite sure why so many of my own lectures have been spiced with Dr. Luffenfluff's little nuggets. I do know my students have been overheard in the hallway saying about me, "Can you believe that guy? He must have run into a real Scholar when he was in school."

§

Fable 20 – Dumb

While it is generally understood that students talk about their teachers out of class, it may not be well recognized that the second favorite hobby of professors is to talk about their students in the faculty cafeteria. In each case, the appraisal of those persons selected for discussion is likely to be unkind. I am reluctant to divulge a recent faculty cafeteria conversation that deteriorated to a contest about the dumbest things students have said in class, but here goes.

Dr. Patricia Plankton told the following story:

"I had a student in one of those big lecture courses who had missed most of the classes. She failed the first two tests and the midterm. I had to wait more than a week to catch her in class and try to raise her level of consciousness about the possible grade she might expect if she didn't do well on the final. 'Hey, no problem,' she told me. 'My sister is in this class and I'll just get the notes from her.'

"'That's fine,' I said, satisfied I had done my duty, but I knew her sister hadn't been in class for a month."

Mr. Philip Coweslip was next:

"There was this lanky, muscle-bound young man who simply could not make a grade higher than 20 points below the next lowest grade in the class on any test or paper. I invited him to the office for a conference and found he could speak no better than he could write. I was surprised to learn he wasn't even on an athletic scholarship.

"In all, I could conclude nothing other than the fellow had a grey-matter problem ... a serious deficiency. After a few moments of semi-conversation, I suggested he consider entering a trade such as plumbing. He said he was trying to get his B.S. in mechanical engineering so he could do just that."

Dr. Ginger Dillinger told this one:

"A classically ditzy coed said she worried about having failed a class. Would she have to take it again? 'If it's a required

When professors talk about their students
in the faculty cafeteria, the appraisal of those persons
selected for discussion is likely to be unkind.

course, you certainly will,' I told her.

"'But I enrolled for the class by mistake.'

"Do you mean it isn't a requirement in your program?

"'It is a requirement,' she said, 'but I had already taken the class.'

"You mean you sat through a class for an entire term and you had already taken the class and you didn't realize it?

"'I thought I had taken it before, but I wasn't sure because the teacher wasn't the same.'

"Well, if it's a required class you just have to take it until you pass it.

"'But I passed it the first time,' she said. 'I made a B in it.'"

Dr. Matt Gracklespat took exception with the maxim that there are no dumb questions with this winning series from a recent Poetry 301 class he teaches:

"Students, my favorite writer of the 19th century is Poe."

Hand goes up.

"Yes?"

"Is your favorite 19th century writer really the Pope?"

"No, it's Poe, P-O-E."

"But is Poe your favorite 19th century writer?"

"Yes."

"Is the 19th century really in the 1800s?"

"Yes."

"Thank you."

Ms. Myra Beguilia won "best dumb answer" from her government class:

"Why did Senator McCarthy accuse liberals of being Communist sympathizers?"

Eager hand shoots up: "He was from Wisconsin!"

Dr. Yolanda Elhambra took the prize for "least insightful comment" from her beginning Spanish class:

"You know," the student observed aloud, "many of the Spanish words we learn are really taken from American words, like 'automobile,' 'telephone' and 'no.'"

The prize for "awkward revelations" was from Mrs. Helen Yellin's intro speech class:

"I was fine when I practiced in front of my bathroom mirror, but when I did it for my girlfriend's sorority sisters, like nothing came out."

Award for "best failed coup attempt" went to Dr. Igor Rigor for this soliloquy from a student in his graduate management seminar:

"Since you're new to the school, Dr. Rigor, I think I should point out that the custom here is not to actually have midterm or final exams. Our professors generally base their grades on our term papers. So while you come here as an endowed, tenured, full professor, we must insist that you follow our graduate program's tradition not to give tests, and I believe my classmates are behind me 100 percent on this."

Although I won no prizes in cafeteria discussion that day, I am keeping my list. I'm going for "most unbelievable excuse given after missing a test when the test wasn't given but the student was too dumb to find that out before embarrassing himself."

§

Fable 21 – Consultants

In this modern age of personality profiling, with more dating sites than news sites on the Internet, no wonder consultants are thriving. Fill out a short biographical sketch and a computer runs the statistics to match your scale scores with those that identify your perfect mate. When such wildly imaginative possibilities become acceptable in love, then marketing, psychology and economics, consultants flourish.

Really, I have nothing against consultants. The term can be a useful synonym for "unemployed" as in "Well, right now I'm consulting." But I do resent the former faculty member who develops one measly little scale, becomes a career consultant and thinks she knows everything.

Dr. Lilly Pigenpech personified the type. She had spent her dissertation years developing and honing a 20-question corporate employee satisfaction test. After 10 years as an associate professor of management, she had published several scholarly articles on the Pigenpech Satisfaction Scale and began getting gigs from companies that wanted her to assess their employees.

She quickly realized that the organizations most interested in her services were those in which workers formed the largest block of corporate expense. For example, a firm that produced widgets had 80 percent of its expenses tied up in the raw materials, manufacturing equipment and distribution of widgets. But a "service" organization that produced nothing tangible had 80 percent of its expenses tied up in employees, and in this regard universities were the ultimate nothing producers. She quit her teaching job and went into full-time consulting for universities.

Dr. Pigenpech had the ideal background for assessing faculty satisfaction. She hired interns to administer and analyze the satisfaction scale and kept herself free to make outcome presentations to the higher administration. Here is how such a

"My research shows there is nothing you can do to satisfy this group," Dr. Pigenpech said. "So it's better to do nothing for them at all."

$25,000 session went at one of the sprawling West Coast state universities.

"Fully 50 percent of your faculty members can be classified in what we term the Disgruntled, Outspoken and Grumbling category, the DOGs as we like to call them," Dr. Pigenpech intoned. "They are unhappy, disillusioned and will denounce the institution every chance they get."

"Good grief," the chancellor exclaimed. "Fully half of our faculty are mad DOGs. Are we in trouble? Are we going to lose half our teaching faculty to other schools?"

"Oh, you are definitely in trouble," the consultant explained. "You are in trouble because you're not going to lose them. They will stay with you until they retire or are carried out of the classroom."

"What can we do to make them content?"

"My research has shown there is nothing you can do to satisfy this group. Give 'em raises, they're unhappy with the amount. Reduce their teaching load, cut their office hours, contribute to their coffee klatch fund … nothing seems to help. So it's better to do nothing for them at all.

"We've done that for them already," the president said.

"And it didn't help, did it. Moving on, you have another 33 percent of faculty we call the PIPs for Positive, Interested and Participating. The perky PIPs are your bread-and-butter employees who come to class with a smile and a prepared lecture. They advise students, do their research and serve cheerfully on committees."

"How can we increase our PIPs?" the chairman asked.

"No, you should be asking how you can afford to replace them," Dr. Pigenpech replied. "Their bubbly spirit and star potential is bound to be recognized every time they interact with peers at national conferences. These are the academic nomads who will get attractive job offers at better schools. When you have to replace them, it will cost you at least 20 percent more in salary plus a new computer, and you have only a one-third chance of getting someone as good as the PIP you're losing."

"How can we keep them?" the dean asked.

"You could reward them annually with significant raises," Dr. Pigenpech suggested.

"Moving on," the president said.

"You have another 12 percent of faculty who just go through the motions. We call them Disoriented, Unengaged and Hollow, the zombie DUHs."

"You mean they don't do anything?" the provost asked.

"Look at it in a good way," Dr. Pigenpech said encouragingly, "They don't do anything bad. Many are near retirement, although some are still in their early 30s and have recently earned tenure. On the one hand, they don't move the program along; on the other hand, they don't impede it."

"Can we motivate them to activity?" the dean asked.

"I wouldn't try. The best you could do is to turn them into DOGs, and I say let sleeping dogs lie, don't you agree?"

"How can we identify them?" the chairman asked.

"You know them already," Dr. Pigenpech said. "They are the quiet ones at faculty meetings. They bring their own lunch to the faculty dining room. They play Mozart symphonies in their offices and whistle along with the melody."

"That explains a lot," the chairman admitted.

"Finally, 5 percent of your faculty can be classified as Berserk, Outraged and Paranoid, the batty BOPs. They see conspiracy behind every new policy and are quick to challenge it publicly. These are the ones who write letters to the editor, carry signs at demonstrations and try to organize campus protests."

"We have our list," the president said.

"What do we do about the BOPs?" the dean asked.

"Keep 'em agitated," Dr. Pigenpech advised.

"They're already agitated," the chancellor said.

"Don't let up. If it weren't for the BOPs, the university would sink into a dull, stolid morass of complacency. As managers of this institution of higher education, it is your duty to dream up new policies and procedures guaranteed to keep the BOPs on their feet and gyrating."

"Out of curiosity," the president inquired, "how do our faculty satisfaction profiles compare with those in the real work world?"

"Interesting question," Dr. Pigenpech said. "My research for corporations shows the percentages are exactly the same."

"Thank you for your insightful report."

Appreciative applause; unobtrusive hand-off of check-enclosed envelope.

Well, actually I don't resent the former faculty member who promotes a measly little scale into a profitable consulting career. I'm just jealous.

§

Fable 22 – The Secret

I now bestow on you the secret to success in college. This is The Secret, the answer you won't find in college guides or in the hushed whispers roommates share after the dorm lights are extinguished. The Secret is selective reading: Read what your professors have written and read their resumes.

Of course, no one would suggest a student should read everything a professor has written. That is too much to expect or stomach even for the professors. Most professors have never re-read anything they've written, with the possible exception of their previous year's lecture notes just before each subsequent class. But clever students will selectively read their professors' writings, knowing such information can yield more course credits than reading the textbook. The further one advances in college, the more valid The Secret, but its benefits accrue even to freshmen.

Gwendolyn Olin was preparing a paper for her freshman biology class when a link on the Internet site led her to a journal article written by her own teacher, Dr. Valerie Mallory. It seemed to embody the core of the very assignment Gwen was researching, so she liberally lifted material from it. Her insights on the topic greatly impressed Dr. Mallory, who found the phrasing in the paper enchanting, as well. It flowed so naturally, just as she might have said it herself. She gave it an "A-plus" and looked favorably on Miss Olin's work the rest of the semester.

Douglas Dinkle, a college sophomore, was looking up Teddy Roosevelt on Wikipedia (a more efficient approach to researching term papers than reading biographies) when he mistakenly accessed the vita of Dr. Shelby Ropsflush, his own political science teacher. Dinkle printed out the page for future reference and reviewed it during class. Dr. Ropsflush played into his hands only three days later while lecturing on the Constitution:

"The Constitutional Convention took place in Philadelphia in 1787 …." Dr. Ropsflush droned.

"Sir," Dinkle's hand shot up, "isn't Philadelphia located in southeastern Pennsylvania?"

It was not the most off-the-wall question Ropsflush had ever been asked in class, but it ranked right up there with the top contenders.

"Yes, that's correct," he replied.

"Then it must be close to Willow Grove?"

"Why, yes, very close," Dr. Ropsflush said as a strange sensation warmed him all over.

"I grew up in Willow Grove," Dinkle continued, "although I was just a little boy when we left there, but I'll never forget those chilly winters and the smell of hot cocoa from the kitchen stove. The spring was my favorite time. We'd play sandlot baseball and have cookouts …." And Dinkle went on with these vague, nostalgic references to "Anytown USA" for nearly five minutes while Dr. Ropsflush listened wistfully and longed for those trouble-free days of his own youth in Willow Grove, Pa.

When the boy ran out of Norman Rockwell-type allusions to his days in Willow Grove, he sat down. Dr. Ropsflush remained silent for a moment. "Dinkle … isn't it?" he asked in a voice choked with emotion. He could not finish the lecture. He went back to his office and spent the rest of the day reminiscing over his high school yearbook through teary eyes. Frequently that semester he called Dinkle at night just to chat about their mutual hometown. Dr. Ropsflush felt no compunction when he raised the lad's course grade a little, from a "D" to an "A." Had it not been for political science and physical education, Dinkle might have spent the rest of his life in the Navy.

Mary McCrary, a graduate business student, completed her thesis, "A Vindication of the Clabberwane Theories," in which she proved beyond reasonable doubt that Clabberwane's work ultimately triumphed, while his colleagues at the Zurich School of Finance – from which he had been ejected in public disgrace – were only jealous of his superior intellect. At least Dr. Edgar Clabberwane, her major professor, had no reasonable doubt, and he secured Mary a post-graduate fellowship.

The only thing to be wary of in applying The Secret of selective reading is to read thoroughly enough. Don't fall into the trap that cost Benjamin Boronsky his "A" in Dr. Hellstrom's anthropology class.

Boronsky was doing his senior term paper on the aborigines of Ecuador. He selected the topic after reading a brief passage under Dr. Hellstrom's picture in the back of the faculty handbook that heralded his professor as a leading scholar on Ecuadorian anthropology. Following clues from reading the plaques and certificates hanging on Dr. Hellstrom's office walls, Boronsky found that his professor had done considerable research on the aborigines of Ecuador back when he was a graduate student in Michigan. Boronsky located two obscure journal articles and a literature review his professor had done at the time.

Impishly, the student used his professor's themes in the senior paper and drew the same conclusions.

Dr. Hellstrom read the paper and became furious. He decided to make an example of Boronsky in front of the class the next day. It went something like this:

"Class, we have a young man who has neither been to Ecuador nor, as I read his work, has bothered to find it on the map," Dr. Hellstrom began. "In fact, this pretender has alleged that a tribe of Ecuadorian aborigines built a coastal city that was destroyed by a massive earthquake. I don't want to name any names, but he's the second from the left on the third row," Hellstrom pointed at Boronsky and sneered.

"My own research," Hellstrom continued, his voice rising, "has shown this to be a lie perpetrated against the unsuspecting anthropological community by some unscrupulous fraud whose ignorant gibberish Boronsky here has treated as gospel," he shouted. He stood over Boronsky as he finished, "Young man, your entire paper is refuted by a dig I led just three years ago, and it's all right here in my recent book!" he roared, and he let the book fall on Boronsky's head.

The student's error was evident. Dr. Hellstrom had forgotten he published the articles some 20 years before and didn't

"Young man, your entire paper is refuted by a dig
I led just three years ago, and it's all right here
in my recent book!" he roared.

remember he was the unscrupulous fraud of whom he had spoken in class. Boronsky couldn't very well say he had used Hellstrom's work, so he took his "C-minus" without comment.

Actually, Dr. Hellstrom hadn't remembered his former treatises about the Ecuadorian aborigines because he had borrowed those early notions from another's work, that of his own professor, Dr. Gustov Gusuntheit, who had written the articles based on work he had encountered some 20 years before.

§

Fable 23 – 6th Period

Perhaps it has happened to you. It seemed to happen to me virtually every year of college, and with me it even began in high school.

I'm talking about a phenomenon called "6th Period," or at least it was called that in high school. I got 6th Period Gym class, but nobody told me what that meant until it was too late.

We were a scrawny group as we dressed out in the locker room and ran to the practice field ready to play a little tag football, or so we thought. We were milling around on the field when our teacher, the varsity football coach, came out of the varsity locker room with his whistle. Lumbering after him was the meat locker of the high school: Guys who stood six-foot and beyond; whose thighs were larger than my waist; who had no necks whatsoever; whose every head either wore spiked mohawks or was shaved bald. It was the varsity team.

They lined up in front of us on the field as the coach stood at the sidelines and blew his whistle. I heard someone say "hike," and the next two seconds sounded like a buffalo stampede interspersed with the snaps of broken bones. The team had scored a touchdown, although it was more of a tribute to the quarterback's fancy footwork in being able to step over so many awkwardly strewn bodies.

This was 6th Period Gym. To clarify, the varsity football team had study hall 5th period and used the time to dress out and butt their heads against the steel pilings of the building. After limbering up, it was time for practice, and the boys who got 6th Period Gym were the opposing squad for the entire semester or their admission to surgery, whichever came first.

We were simply no contest for them, nor did we try to be. We heard the whistle, stiffened with the word "hike," and ran for the sidelines if we could. I was supposed to block the center, a 350-pound farm boy named "Hog" who had to be led to school on a chain. Every time I heard "hike," I attempted to dig a hole

I was supposed to block the center, a 350-pound farm boy. Every time I heard "hike," I tried to dig a hole and crawl in it.

and crawl in it. The coach caught me and lectured me in front of the whole team.

"Do you think this is some sort of game? Have you no school spirit? What kind of Toad are you?" Our school mascot was Timmy the Toad.

Sixth Period Gym proved to be a lesson in self-preservation. We prayed for rainy days and submitted a lot of doctors' excuses.

Then came college, and I found out 6th Period could be any time at all. For example, my freshman geology class should have been a dead giveaway. It was held in a huge lecture hall, and as I peered down the curved row of dark-haired male students to my left I noticed every eye was slanted; the same to my right. In fact, three-quarters of the students were Asians, which I thought was pretty peculiar for a Southern land-grant university bordering the Gulf of Mexico. I should have known something was up when our professor, Dr. Wong, began:

"We will skip the igneous, sedimentary, metamorphic, feldspar, mica and crystalline quartz. I will also assume you have committed the paleontology chart to memory. So we will begin with organic chemistry's relation to the fossils in layers of shale, about which you are most interested."

I wasn't. And not until after midterm did I find out this was the section of freshman geology normally reserved for foreign exchange scholarship students to the region's premier department of petrochemical geology – there to learn how to discover oil. Unfortunately, the drop date had already passed. I didn't.

But my sophomore section of University Chorus was glorious. Nearly 250 voices singing in unison and every one of them capable of solo. Well, almost every one. I got in by being able to sing "la, la, la" in tune with three notes played on the piano. I felt such an audition might have qualified me for a campfire sing-along or karaoke after a pub crawl, but not for 6th Period University Chorus where we gave public performances of Handel's Messiah, the "Hallelujah Chorus," and still had time for other light ditties in Russian and Italian. I got by mouthing the words and using expressive hand gestures. The director had to insist I control myself.

"It's all right to get into the music," he said, "but we've already selected the soloists, and you're just part of the baritone section. Stop trying to show off."

I had a recurring nightmare the whole semester that we would be on stage and every other singer would stop on cue, leaving me open-mouthed and restraining my hand gestures. But I wore my dark suit and tie to the performance and narrowly escaped passing out from stage fright when the curtain went up.

I never missed practice. Once past the "la, la, la" qualifying test, the grade in University Chorus was based solely on attendance. I finally got my 6th Period "A."

§

Fable 24 – Big Words

Once there was a teacher – we'll call her Dr. Edith Bitty – who followed a solitary motto all her life: Never use a little word when a multi-syllabic word will do.

She had not always been Dr. Edith Bitty. As a child she was just Edie Bitty, a shy lass of diminutive proportions who didn't learn to speak until she was nearly 4 years old. It is unknown if her name, her size or her late leap into communication caused her to be enamored of large words. But when she did speak, her vocabulary greatly astonished both family and friends.

On the playground, when other girls were playing jump rope, she declined saying merely, "I hesitate to depreciate your hempen avocation, but I am apprehensive about potential abrasions to my patella." Those few girls who would play with her spoke slowly, assuming she was French.

But Edie Bitty led a rather normal life, with the exception of one recurring fantasy. She believed her special guardian angel, Mary the Vocabulary Fairy, visited her at night and whispered lexicon in her ear, along with etymology, definition, pronunciation and synonymy. "It's a gift," Mary would tell her, "Use it wisely 'cause there are no others."

Her schooling was impaired by the gift. Some of her teachers thought well of Edie and were impressed with her superior vocabulary. They wondered why she was not a "straight-A" student. But some thought Edie was an impudent blowhard because her coursework was not equal to the exaggerated manner of speaking they believed she affected. These were the ones who contributed most to her lack of "A's."

Her parents worried. Oh, they had learned to carry a dictionary, but they saw how difficult it was for Edie to get along with peers. They wondered if she would be able to cope later in life. So they took her to a psychologist who interviewed Edie and took copious notes (which he later discarded as too difficult to decipher).

Edie believed her special guardian angel,
Mary the Vocabulary Fairy, visited her at night
and whispered lexicon in her ear.

The question was: How can a person with a gift for unintelligible gab make the most of it? Edie Bitty seemed suited for only a few professions. She could be an insurance claims form writer. She could become a mortgage loan officer at a bank or she could write government documents. But the avenue of widest potential, in fact a boulevard, was for her to become a college professor in virtually any field of her choosing. Everyone seemed pleased with this last option and Edie Bitty, who really wowed the teachers in her graduate seminars (where an impressive vocabulary is just about all you need), became Dr. Edith Bitty, professor of economics, a near-perfect choice.

Students in the large sophomore sections of Macro Economics 203 found her lectures less than lucid. For instance, one of the brighter students in her class jotted these notes on deficit spending:

"Nations requiring more abundant pecuniary liquidity than previously allocated taxable revenues ... frequently decide to ... and it is becoming more prevalent today."

A lesser student just jotted, "Huh?"

The entire semester was a learning disaster, although a few ingenious students barely passed by relying heavily on the textbook. Interestingly, Dr. Bitty's student evaluations showed great respect – almost reverence – for her as a teacher. One of the brighter students wrote on the form:

"Dr. Bitty is the most impressive, inspiring pedagogue I have had at this university."

A lesser student jotted, "Like, she was awesome, you know, but I got really confused sometimes, you know?"

Her department colleagues were also greatly impressed, but the chairman worried that she was too deep for students to grasp. He questioned if college teaching was the correct vocation for Dr. Bitty. Would he have to fire her at tenure time? He brought her in for a personnel evaluation conference.

"Dr. Bitty, I'm concerned about your long-term contentment in the classroom."

Obviously, this chairman had been around awhile and probably had attended a weekend administrator's workshop.

Rather than express potentially confrontational convictions to faculty such as, "I think it's time for you to retire," he preferred the glass-is-half-full approach such as, "Don't you miss fishing?" Rather than saying, "Don't bother turning your pay envelope upside down and shaking it at the next merit raise period," he might say, "In this economic environment, moving your family from its trailer might be premature." Instead of threatening, "I'm going to schedule you for 8 a.m. classes six days a week next semester," he would say, "You should really try to get more rest." His euphemism for "I won't be renewing your contract" was "I worry that your faculty office may be too small to suit you."

But Dr. Bitty countered his challenge about her teaching fitness by replying, "Your apprehension is categorically unfounded. Apprentices under my tutelage deliberate every pronouncement I articulate, making the experience an indubitable source of gratification."

When she left his office, she felt she had stated her position in no uncertain terms, but was unsure if her point had been understood.

It was true Dr. Bitty didn't belong in college teaching. There was actually only one position at the university made to order for someone with her communication inclinations, something the higher administration had recognized in her immediately. Her chairman could not fire her at tenure time because she was named to that position. She had become his dean.

§

Fable 25 – Enrollment

Overpopulation used to be as frightening a specter as nuclear war, juvenile delinquency or the heartbreak of psoriasis. But today overpopulation wouldn't even make it on the minor telethon circuit. In fact, the overpopulation lobby did so well in the 1960s that in these baby boomer grandchildren years, U.S. universities face just the opposite problem: declining enrollments.

The predicament has reached epic proportions. How do you retire that $40 million dormitory building bond debt with no students? How do you continue to get larger tax appropriations or solicit funds from rich alumni for student centers when there are no students to center? And worst of all, how do you maintain the salaries of tenured faculty whose classes are empty?

Betsy Ross College, a small liberal arts institution in Indiana, was facing just such a problem. Its board of directors predicted eminent bankruptcy if they didn't do something immediately to make "Old Drudge" (as its graduates fondly referred to their alma mater) more appealing to students. The board had lowered the entrance standards to accommodate even the basket cases of academic prowess, but had been forced to increase annual tuition fees to $20,000 as the head count continued to dwindle. Betsy Ross's prospects were flagging; her demise seemed dyed in the wool; it appeared she hadn't a stitch of time left. In desperation, the board hired one Smitty Penderghast, a hotshot from a New York City public relations agency, as its new president.

Smitty kept his talons on the nation's pulse. His solution was to reverse admission requirements, to make Betsy Ross the country's most difficult college to get into. The first year ended in near-suicide. Enrollments dropped to only one-tenth of the student body as Betsy Ross ridded itself of academic debris. If faculty members had not pitched in by holding car washes and bake sales in their abundant spare time, Betsy Ross would have flown at half-staff.

But by the second year, word was getting out. High school seniors who had been accepted by Yale and Stanford were rejected by Betsy Ross College. Smitty accepted applicants of far lesser academic portend, to be sure, but to boost the college's image, he cared enough to reject the very best.

The high school counselor rumor mill was abuzz. This little college in rural Indiana was really tough to get into … it must be good. Enrollment doubled and then doubled again, and just to ensure it kept happening, Smitty made an occasional reject of a Vanderbilt, Brown or Caltech acceptance. Then, just when things were going so well, the former public relations expert went amuck.

Smitty had visions of building an empire. He changed the school's name to "Horizon University" … and enrollment doubled again.

He convinced the board to drop the school's liberal arts emphasis and offer more career-related programs. The following are examples from a recent catalogue:

Bachelor of Arts in Salad Bar Management. Meet new friends as you munch your way through life's little garnishes. Classes in celery slicing, cherry tomato polishing and sneeze-guard cleanup. Profit decisions related to skimping on artichoke hearts, asparagus spears and marinated mushroom caps (prerequisite, Economics I).

Bachelor of Science in Pizza Delivery. Fun in the fast lane begins with this rewarding career. Learn detoxifying principles for delivering anchovy specials. Manual dexterity a must for two-wheel cornering, warmer-box thermostat setting and using belt-slung change makers (prerequisite, reliable vehicle). Master's available in pizza dough tossing.

Smitty put in individual courses with titles he dreamed up himself: Fond of Forensics; Antics with Semantics; Get Down Ghetto Blaster Repair; Close Encounters with Microbiology; and It Came from Western Europe. Enrollments doubled again

Smitty convinced the board to drop the school's liberal arts emphasis and offer more career-related programs.

and there would have been no end to Smitty's selling of the university had it not been for his Bachelor's of Fine Arts in Gorilla Suit and Belly Gram Birthday Greetings.

The details are far too sordid to divulge, but it is proper to concede that the dowager director of the board of trustees was indeed surprised by what jumped out of her cake at the foundation's annual banquet and birthday party through some minor confusion in orders at the fine arts department.

A full investigation by the remaining board members forced Smitty Penderghast's resignation and the dismantling of his innovative programs that had led the university to capacity enrollments in these troubled times. The dowager is rumored to be living with a rather hairy 20-year-old former student at her secluded villa outside Gary, Ind., overlooking the lake.

§

Fable 26 – Publish

Those who can, do. Those who can't do, teach. Those who can't teach, publish.

The most recent addition to the old platitude, courtesy of teachers who rarely publish, is the scourge of the higher education profession. Universities that seek prestige and increased grant monies pay only lip service to teaching while paying cash for faculty research and publication (the lip is generous; the cash parsimonious). Even college professors can discern how the system allocates rewards.

Dr. Wanda Funderbinder was told early. She had earned her master's in European history. For her doctorate, she specialized in European wars of the 18th century and remembered the words of her mentor, the renowned Dr. Bunkman Debukee, who told her there were three kinds of faculty members:

1) The auditorium lecturer, who would be ridiculed by peers as a "performer" – a stand-up comedian with a stage but no cover charge – and there might be only one or two such individuals per university. Students would fill their classes for whatever they presented. Some might actually impart information.

2) The teacher, who serves as the base of the totem pole of success in the professorial ranks. Teachers would rank higher, since they comprise the widest spectrum of university faculty, but at the better universities (that purge those who can't teach at all) no one ranks below the teacher.

3) Researchers and publishers. They ARE the totem pole, and they range from crouching rabbits at the bottom to spread-winged eagles at the top.

"A good teacher," Debukee informed Wanda, "might be lucky enough to win an Outstanding Teaching Award after 20 years and be given a gold watch. Look at my wrist," Debukee said, pulling up his sleeve, and Wanda saw that her mentor wore no watch. A stunning but valuable lesson.

She received her degree and landed a job at a decent

Researchers and publishers ARE the totem pole,
and they range from crouching rabbits at the bottom
to spread-winged eagles at the top.

university, one of those medium-stature, Midwestern schools. The first year was brutal as she prepared four classes a semester. It was all she could do to have a lecture ready for the next day of each class. And her ability to do work in her office was hindered by the teacher who shared the suite: Dr. Ida Whippleschmidt.

Whippleschmidt was associate-professor-going-for-full, and a meaner breed of cat does not exist. She had been passed over in her last promotion attempt a year before, and she realized the only thing worse than being an associate-professor-going-for-full was being an associate professor. It had changed her whole personality. When a student came into her suite asking for advice and interrupting preparation for her next journal article, Whippleschmidt would snap, "My office hours are posted on the door, and I'm not in until then." But when "then" arrived, she had left minutes before. Her students sought help from Wanda, and in a short time Wanda had quite a lengthy list of advisees and confidants.

While a few faculty members find solace and even pleasure in being friendly with students, almost no one finds any redeeming value in serving on committees. Wanda made a fatal error one afternoon when the history department faculty was debating the annual picnic and stalled for about two hours on the question of potato salad or cole slaw. In frustration she lost all perspective and shouted, "Give it to committee!"

They did, after the chairman appointed her committee head. Then she served on the curriculum board, the library holdings advisory counsel, Reduce Paper Waste Task Force, the Awards Banquet Menu Committee (where she made no friends by recommending fried chicken a second year in a row) and a host of other terribly time-consuming departmental service groups.

"When," she asked her chairman, "am I going to find time to do some research and publishing?"

"Very soon, I hope," the chairman said, "because you come up for tenure in two more years."

So Wanda spent her early morning hours and weekends in the library perusing writings in her specialty of European wars. And a disaster followed. She found herself deviating from her prepared class lecture to share with students a tidbit she had read about Napoleon's rumored paramour on the Russian retreat who died of frostbite to an unmentionable. The details of the trip were quite interesting and more than a little titillating. The class listened three minutes after the bell rang.

Wanda fell into the same trap several more times that semester and was shocked to find all her classes over-enrolled the next term, which meant more papers to grade and more students to advise. Students were talking with her at the end of class and trailing her to her office. Wanda was becoming a teacher and recognized it as the kiss of death. She called her mentor long-distance.

Debukee told her to put an end to it immediately. At all costs. Her career in education was on the line. "Do you want to be assistant to the local branch library director this time next year?" he asked. It was warning enough.

"Class," she informed her students the next day, "I have decided to cover more material from the textbook." She opened the text and read to them for the remainder of the course, and she did that in all her classes except by the end of the semester she told the remaining two students to just buy the CD.

Committee work ended abruptly when she recommended fried chicken for the banquet a third year in a row, suggesting also that it be brought in from a local greasy spoon take-out.

But Wanda worried about her student advisees. They were her friends, her charges. She could not just Whippleschmidt them. It was a quandary that caused her much concern. What could she do that would not hurt their feelings, would be educationally beneficial and would get them out of her office?

She invited them all to meet with her from that time forward, whenever they wished, at her cubicle in the history section of the university library. She gave each a small sketched map of where the building was located.

Wanda Funderbinder received tenure and later served on Whippleschmidt's promotion committee when her suite mate came up for the third time.

§

Fable 27 – Quantitative Grading

"That grading system is best which allows a teacher to give a student the grade he or she actually deserves." I heard that somewhere, but it is more than a fact. It's a universal principle that guards teachers from open attack.

College professors are symbols of authority, the personification of dignity and figureheads around whom the cloak of wisdom is wrapped to the point of near suffocation. The professor works for honor and pride-in-accomplishment, certainly not the money. So when this noble personage is approached by some sniveling student who claims to have made a "B" on every exam and paper throughout the semester and would like to know just why he received a "C-plus" in the course, a crisis exists that threatens the foundations of American education.

The omnipotent professor must have a reply prepared in advance of such onslaughts. Responses range from the obvious to the opaque. Many professors use the standard, archaic explanations distributed annually in the back pages of several professional journals:

- "Your attitude was an important factor."
- "Attendance is something I demand."
- "Those who choose to sit in the back of the room have made their position clear from the first day of class."
- "I would love to discuss this with you further. Come see me during spring break."

But teachers who rely on such slippery qualitative methods are open to challenge. Today, the advent of statistics allows the truly outstanding professor – the model educator – to use a more precise technique guaranteed to satisfy as it mystifies.

At the first class meeting, the outstanding teacher outlines the grading system for the semester in a way that will be clearly

A younger student asks, "When you said 'weighed,' did you mean applying another grading scale or by the pound?"

understood by all. It might go something like this:

"Good morning, class. My grade book is now open before you, and I feel it is only fair to inform you that anything you say may be held against you at judgment day ... falling on May 5th this semester.

"You will be graded on a point count-percentage-adjusted, sliding-cumulative-deductive-shifting-transfer scale that will later be put on a curve. At any and every moment during the semester, you will know precisely what your grade in this class is."

The professor pauses to be certain all are taking notes, sitting erect, looking straight ahead and still in the room.

"Now take this down. You will be responsible for two book reports, a term paper, a class presentation, a panel discussion and a reading list. These assignments will constitute 63 percent of your final grade, so if you do just this much you are fairly guaranteed at least a 'D.'

"Class attendance will be counted as 4 percent, with a .5 percent deduction for cutting during mid-week and 1.3 percent deducted for cutting on a day adjacent to the weekend.

".7 percent will be added to your total for every intelligent question you ask in class. I encourage this unless I determine you are only trying for points, in which case I deduct .3 percent.

"Your notes in this course will be taken up periodically, carefully weighed and returned with a grade indicative of your class standing at exactly that time."

A younger student interrupts. "When you said 'weighed,' did you mean applying another grading scale or by the pound?"

Soft chuckles follow.

"Miss Dinwimple, isn't it?" the professor inquires. "That's minus .3 percent."

Chuckles cease abruptly, and the professor continues.

"Now to ensure that the overall class grades are distributed properly, your individual average will be compared with that of the class as a whole to derive a proper mean from which your standard deviation will be calculated to yield your final grade."

An older student can't help himself. "When you said 'mean,' were you referring to the arithmetic average or the grading attitude in this class?"

"Very good," Mr. Flackswax. "Class attitude is an essential element in my grading system. I call it the FLIP grade: F for foul, L for lax; I for irritating; P for pigheaded. An otherwise passing grade could get FLIPed by the end of class. That's plus .7 percent for you.

"Other matters will be scaled with the same deft precision as they arise. You may now leave to think about what I've said, and remember, the drop date will be upon us soon."

Thus the modern professor is armed with the necessary ammunition to rebuke the most aggrieved assailant at grading time. When the "C-plus" student makes the plea, this teacher merely replies:

"Miss Dinwimple, your grade at the last day of the semester was an 81. However, after your grade was FLIPed you had a 78.43, a 'C-plus.' Good day."

§

Fable 28 – Majors

While these chapters attempt to deal only with irrefutable documented facts, the following transcript of an audiotape contains information so edifying it will be presented without further verification of particulars. Actually, the tape received considerable inquiry by the district attorney because when it became public, the dean of men, dean of women, and the vice president of academics at Rusty Thornton University all disappeared without a trace. The incident has been called "Rustygate," and some portions of the tape are simply too raw for public scrutiny.

The only voice on the tape is alleged to be that of Dr. Ollie Sinkwell, dean of men at Thornton University, talking to the dean of women, the vice president of academics and possibly some other individuals who may still be employed at Thornton.

This 18-minute portion of the tape, presented without editing, contains Dr. Sinkwell's views on the kinds of individuals associated with various academic programs at Thornton:

"Well, if you think those others are strange majors, consider the psych department. People major in psychology because they think they're nuts. They hope they'll find out how to cure themselves before they do something they'll regret. Their four-year tuition is cheaper than seeing an analyst for the same four years, but they don't realize that all their teachers went into psychology for the same reason, and it didn't help them. [knowing snickers heard]

"And how about those computer science majors? Why don't they ever bathe or change their clothes? True, the computers don't complain, but no one else can stand to go into the computer labs. We ought to program those machines so every week they flash a message like, 'Warning: A skunk died here during the night. Just to be on the safe side, go get cleaned up. We'll talk again later.' [embarrassed light titter fading away]

"What I really find pathetic is those kids in the education

school. I mean, have you seen those college entrance scores? You can't rub two of them together and get an I.Q. They just want to help young people learn, and they're so nice until they've been teaching about five years and then they grow horns and pointy tails. You really can't blame 'em 'cause they're facing another 35 years of the same thing before they can retire. [gratuitous spiteful chortles]

"But the scary place is the science building. I won't even go in there for a donor reception. Those chemistry majors, every one of them since the age of 8 playing with their little chemistry sets trying to make a bomb, and ten years of practice since. Bunch of crazies if you ask me. What are all those squiggly little formulas they write? Must be some kind of secret code. [some mumbling, possibly about national security]

"At least you know what the creepy chemists are up to. If we're counting Machiavellian majors, take a walk to the speech department. The teachers over there – whoa, don't even get me started on speech teachers, those smug passive-aggressive thespian wannabes in high heels and stage makeup, and the women are worse – they grade the students on how smoothly they can lie. Got to be able to argue both sides convincingly, and once the kids catch on you can't stop 'em. The best liars become TV weather forecasters, the worst fake foreign accents and recommend the overpriced dinner specials at fancy restaurants. [resentful rasp "and expect a big tip"]

"I feel sad for the accounting majors, the poor dears. Sure, it's a parent's job to try to encourage their child into a field that virtually guarantees a viable income. But any daddy's boy or girl who caves into becoming an accountant deserves the life they get. Can you imagine a 40-year career behind a computer screen squinting at columns of numbers? I'd rather eat worms. [grunts of heartfelt agreement]

"The performing arts: dance, music, theater, film and poetry. What a bunch of pansy pushovers. One in a hundred has a chance of making a decent living while the other 99 end up trying to get a teaching job. It's a self-fulfilling prophecy designed to perpetuate the misconception that society values

"Those chemistry majors, every one of them playing with their little chemistry sets trying to make a bomb. Bunch of crazies if you ask me."

such nonsense. Give me a business major any day.

"That is, of course, assuming there's a family business. Otherwise, you're a bank teller or a realtor. [nods of agreement, barely audible on the tape]

"The social sciences: history, anthropology, sociology, political science – 'science' my eye, why don't they just call it government? – geography and communication. Those pinhead majors drag carts of textbooks around and think they're actually learning something. First year on the job, they realize it was all a hoax and they'd be better off in the Army. But the social sciences teach them to scoff at any kind of discipline, so they have to join the Peace Corps instead. [whisper of profound sympathy]

"Criminal justice … there's an oxymoron. Since when do you need a college degree to become a cop? Give me the old-school guys anytime, like the ex-cops we hire off the books as security guards to lock down the dorms at night and break up the student rallies and deliver the library-fine cash boxes to the administration building and infiltrate the faculty union and drive our coed escort service girls back to campus and wiretap the president's office …. [dead silence]

§

Fable 29 – Modern History

Any person who makes it past age 50 is likely to exhibit "golleee" moments about innovations regardless of the era in which they live. While we are used to Gramps looking at an iPhone and uttering "golleee," consider the people born in 1865, just as the Civil War ended, and imagine their "golleee" moments when they first saw a Model-T Ford automobile and then an airplane, both occurring in the person's 40s. Or the people born in 1918, as World War One was ending, who witnessed the first moon landing at age 51. Or the World War Two baby boomers who bought their first desktop computer in the mid-1980s, before they turned 40. Golleee! These are marvelous accomplishments in the history of the progress of humankind.

Dr. Terrence "Tiptoe" Tillingham had earned his nickname by getting excited during his Modern History 302 lectures whenever he recounted what he considered a truly golleee moment. He would raise his arms in an evangelical arc and actually rise four or five inches as he spoke, getting just outside the limits of his microphone so he couldn't be heard. It went something like this:

"But the greatest breakthrough, class, and this will surely be on the final exam, was when our former president's brain trust decided that the answer to energy independence was to harness …." and Tiptoe would be out of range, talking to the stars.

Despite their mediocre grades, students adored him. They welcomed the novelty of an animated professor, and they filled the auditorium as if it were an IMAX film on shark attacks. Here is an example of his presentations taken directly from his notes, so they will be audible all the way through:

"Class, there are two modern retail stores that simply astound me. If you could go back to 1970 and tell strangers on the street, nobody would believe you. Of course, the first is Starbucks. Who would have conceived of a $5 cup of coffee,

Consider the people born in 1865, just as the Civil War ended, and imagine their astonishment when they first saw a Model-T Ford and then an airplane.

with people waiting in lines to buy it and another Starbucks on every corner? Unbelievable. And that corrugated piece of cardboard that pops open to form a circular holder so you don't burn your hand. Sheer genius.

"But the other store is even more remarkable, in my opinion. If you said to people in 1970 that there would be two- and three-story-high buildings with 200,000 square feet of air-conditioned retail space and several million dollars worth of inventory and that toddlers and even teens would beg to go there and that these would be bookstores, people would laugh. 'Surely you mean libraries,' they would say. But no, I would tell them, real bookstores that sell mostly books and magazines and have overstuffed chairs and desks and every single chair is occupied by a person reading a book just for enjoyment, golleee, and two other people standing up leaning against the shelves reading a book and waiting for one of the comfortable chairs to come vacant. And they would line up clutching their selections so they could pay $100 or more for an armful of books that they could check out absolutely free in any library. Just amazing."

Some innovations received dubious reviews in his notes:

"Velcro; now who thought that up? Mini skirts; can't complain. Squeeze cheese; oh, please. Four-digit zip code extension after the five-digit zip code; who can remember the other four? Credit cards; a mixed blessing. 3-D; golleee."

Of course, Tiptoe didn't always wax eloquent. He was genuinely puzzled by some modern phenomena, as his notes reveal:

"Punk-rock music ... is it really? Wearing baseball caps with the brim turned backwards ... to ward off neck burns?

"And I just don't understand America's favorite modern sports like NASCAR racing. Guess you have to be there in the thick of things to enjoy the beer and noxious fumes. Ditto for professional wrestling. I remember basketball in high school as good, clean exercise, but nobody came to the games. Then, when I was an undergrad at a Big-10 school in the 1960s, you could attend the basketball games free, and nobody came. But now, wow. Here's a sport reserved for guys with pituitary disorders where people watch an hour-long game for three hours when everything that matters happens in the last two minutes. And golf. It's one thing to play it, but why would you go out in the heat or rain and stand around the greens while people take 10 minutes to plan their putt? Is there anything duller than watching golf on TV? Even the announcers are so embarrassed they can only speak in whispers."

Tiptoe's final lecture was his most memorable. He had discovered what most people would consider a relatively innocuous invention that somehow led him beyond his normal level of exhilaration. It was the last lecture of the last day of the last semester before his mandatory retirement.

"Class, I want to share a recent discovery of mine, something that had never even occurred to me previously but is a wondrous revelation, one for which I am certain you will share my enthusiasm.

"When I was a lad, not much younger than you are today, the favorite graduation gift was a fountain pen. Let me briefly describe the device. It was a beautiful instrument that cost one or two day's pay. You unscrewed the cap and dipped the steel point in a bottle of ink. There was a lever that depressed a rubber diaphragm inside the tube, and you worked the lever back and forth to suction the ink into the cylinder. Then you put the two pieces together, wiped the steel point with a rag or tissue, and it was ready for use. The ink often smeared on the paper and left blotches. It frequently bled through the page and sullied the page behind. The pen point tore the paper. If you made a mistake, you had to start over. If you put it in your pocket, it leaked and indelibly ruined your shirt or trousers.

"And then, my friends, (I can remember the day as if it were yesterday)," he said as he began drawing something from inside his seersucker jacket and holding it aloft in one hand for the class to see.

"Witness the miracle of the twentieth century. I give you the ballpoint pen!" He made his evangelical arc and began to slowly float upward.

"This new little device became available to the public in

dime stores and drug stores across the country." He halted his rise temporarily for effect, then continued to ascend, his voice trembling with reverence.

"Consider the advancement. No more blotches, no messy ink bottles that perpetually tipped over and spilled in a puddle on the desk and then ran onto the carpet. No soiled shirt pockets. It sold for less than a dollar. Scientists and philosophers could write without having to refill their pens. Productivity was increased exponentially." He was leaving the microphone behind.

"Mankind could maintain continuous thought without pause and produce the discoveries we of the modern age …." He was inaudible but continued speaking for another five minutes, a record.

He alighted just as the bell rang, and the instant his heels touched the floor his students rose en masse and applauded him off the stage. Golleee, what a fitting finale for a modern history professor whose lectures were vintage.

§

Fable 30 – Audio-Visual

What a sad situation to prepare for a teaching career all your life and then find out in the classroom that as much as you want to, as much as you've invested, you just can't teach. Maybe this trial-by-fire procedure says something about the system, although I wouldn't suggest anything as drastic as requiring all would-be college teachers to take an education course.

I believe there should be some provision for students – perhaps in the fifth grade as a special exercise in learning about careers – to stand in front of a class at the blackboard and actually try to teach something. It might do wonders for the entire educational system by eliminating those who simply lack the aptitude and who would discover, probably from this experience alone, that they will be as miserable as their charges if given the power to wield the chalk.

A case in point: Cecil Kuebitz, who loved school. He had been a solid "B" student throughout, mostly. In kindergarten he wanted to teach kindergarten; in first grade he wanted to become a first-grade teacher; and so it went until he longed to be a college professor. He was so happy the day he received his doctorate that he sewed leather patches on the elbows of all his jackets including the tuxedo.

Dr. Kuebitz taught communication arts with a specialty in cinema. He had only two years of practical experience (as a theater usher and a kiosk clerk for a 24-hour photo developing lab), but his degrees in film history were from prestigious schools, and he loved going to the movies. Because he was new to the faculty, Kuebitz got the big intro lecture courses in the history of cinema.

Heaven! Well, it might have been, but he began to suspect his teaching methods were less than adequate. For example, students packed his sections the first day of class, but by the second week he saw rows of vacant chairs. He noticed an inexplicable deep red mark, a line that ran horizontally across his forehead. Some investigation revealed the line was an indentation resulting from his head resting on the front edge of the lectern where he had fallen asleep during his own lectures. He couldn't understand it. The material seemed interesting enough when he researched it for his term papers in graduate school.

Kuebitz sensed impending danger to his career as a college professor. He realized that if he had encountered a teacher as boring as himself, he never would have wanted to be a teacher. He was in a dither, which further interfered with his class preparation. He shared his concern with a colleague who confided, "Whenever I'm unprepared for a class in cinema, I just show a movie."

Kuebitz became indignant at the suggestion. "That's a cop-out," he snapped at the man. "I didn't become a teacher just to baby-sit my students."

But the next day at five minutes before class, he set up a projector and showed a film. He was pleased to note his students remained awake even in the darkened hall, and he heard a few of them discussing the film's theme on the way out the door. "Hey," he thought, "maybe this is the answer."

The next semester was a complete about-face. Kuebitz posted fliers around campus, giving the schedule of his class presentations. He added a few audio-visual refinements to improve attention. The house was standing-room-only on opening day. A computer dimmed the lights on cue and trained a spotlight on the orchestra pit where a 12-piece band blared out a current rhythm-and-blues hit. Kuebitz punched another button and a multi-media slide show began, followed by a short film in Dolby wraparound sound with sense- and smell-orama. Next his five-minute DVD lecture played on eight large-screen television sets lined around the lecture hall. For a big finish, there was a laser light show. Students were spellbound. They had to be ejected from the auditorium to make room for the next class viewing.

Kuebitz found he had a flair for arranging these spectaculars. He experimented with overheads, charts and graphs, with

Kuebitz found he had a flair for arranging these spectaculars and began to wear a monocle and carry a gold-tipped pointer.

computer-generated animation and choral groups borrowed from the music department. The expenses were underwritten by commercials he aired between regular course content. He tried trained seals and elephants, a dance ensemble, jugglers, acrobats and a mime. He began to wear a monocle and carry a gold-tipped pointer. Closing class segments included a standing sing-along to "We Are the Champions."

His classes became the most popular on campus. Kuebitz believed he had it made. But when he came up for tenure, his committee sadly delivered the bad news: He was merely entertaining his students, not educating them. While the cinema department appreciated the additional enrollment, his college teaching days were over.

So Kuebitz left the academy. He now operates a tremendously successful national franchise called "Dr. Kuebitz's Kiddie Korner," a preschooler's audio-visual babysitting service that allows mothers to stay for the shows if they wish, for a slight additional hourly fee.

§

Fable 31 – Red-Ink Grading

It is far better to give than to receive, the old motto says, and teachers would certainly agree when it comes to giving grades. But giving grades can be as difficult as earning them. For example, there are two basic ways to grade.

One is to structure the course so each student starts at zero. "Class," the teacher says on the first day, "everyone has a chance to earn an 'A' in here." (Of course, that's not true, but students find it reassuring.) "We'll have chapter quizzes, one term paper, a midterm and final. You will have every opportunity to earn up to 250 points by the end of the semester." In this approach, students bear the burden of building toward a satisfactory grade under a crushing point accumulation load. The demands can be debilitating.

The other approach is to start at the top and work down. "Everyone starts with 250 points!" the teacher declares on the first day. Of course, the problem here is that every test and paper decreases the student's grade. I tried this system once, but in the fourth week a clever young woman said, "Sir, I'm going to stop attending class now and take my 'B.' See ya."

Dr. Bernie "Bloodstain" Blake was an infamous grader. An extremely conscientious chap, he earned his nickname by bathing his students' papers in red ink. Blake was an English grammar teacher who had written his dissertation on prepositions, and he remained fascinated by them throughout his teaching career. He wondered about the comments he overheard his students making in the hallways after he handed back a set of papers. "The guy marked up my paper in red ink! There was so much red, I couldn't read it!"

Blake wondered about the phrase "marked up my paper." When red-inking a student's work, he was under the impression he was marking it down, not up. Maybe this was a colloquialism.

He liked to think that immediately after class his students

would rush to the library and pore over their red-inked papers, perhaps in study groups, discussing the numerous corrections he had noted. At the very least, he hoped students would take their papers back to their dorm rooms and review his marks individually.

But judging from their lack of progress and the crumpled crimson sheets he found in the hall wastebasket, it occurred to him that he might be putting too many red marks on the papers. Maybe the students were overwhelmed, not reviewing the marks carefully and not learning from their mistakes. And if they were not learning, then what was the purpose of his spending countless hours and barrels of red ink? So he decided to ease up (off) in his red marking.

Blake had gotten into the habit of attaching gummed posted notes on those pages with more extensive red-ink corrections for which there was not enough room on the already scarlet pages. Because these notes tended to curl and drop off (he often found them wadded into little balls on the classroom floor), he had stapled them to the pages. As an experiment, he stopped attaching the notes and was pleasantly surprised later when a student actually used "it's" as the verb contraction form.

Next, he refrained from filling the margin of their papers with numbered asterisks referencing the additional sheets he included of corresponding numbered red-ink commentary associated with their errors. One student used "their" correctly as a pronoun; another got the verb agreement form correct following a compound subject as in "Horace and his buddies were out drinking beer."

Such encouraging improvements led Blake to reduce the usual red-ink marks on the papers themselves. At first he restrained himself by marking only the most egregious grammatical errors and letting the rest slide. A few students seemed to learn that "affect" was the verb form and "effect" the noun. This was the kind of unexpected achievement that would have earned any student a minimum "B" in the course despite all other failings throughout the semester.

And then he toyed with his charges by randomly

Judging from his students' lack of progress and the crumpled crimson sheets in the hall wastebasket, perhaps he was putting too many red marks on the papers.

marking only 10 errors regardless of importance. Again he got improvement, so he cut the red-ink to only the first three mistakes he found and was not disappointed with his students' continuing success.

Blake was thrilled with his discovery. His students were learning, and he had time to take his family to the beach. In fact, he had so much time on his hands that he took an evening job as copy editor at the local newspaper for extra income.

It was a good thing, too, because success often leads to excess. He had stopped red-inking the papers entirely and was fired when his students went to the dean to complain about the "Cs" and "Ds" they received on papers that obviously had never been read. Sure, they might have made a few mistakes, but there were no red marks whatsoever. The dean said she had never seen such a blatant failure to meet accepted teaching standards.

And then his editor at the local paper told him he was not being diligent enough in correcting the reporters' articles. "You need to get these writers' attention. What do you think you're here for?" (He had ended a sentence in a preposition.)

So "Bloodstain" went out and bought a dozen red-ink pens.

§

Fable 32 – Endowments

"Be kind to your 'A' students for they will become the university's future teachers. Be kinder to your 'B' students for they will send their children to the university and provide continuing enrollment. But be kindest of all to your 'C' students for they are the ones who will lavish great endowments on the university."

This old maxim, as most of its ilk, seems just cruel enough to be true. How many former Rhodes Scholars are today reading their poetry to pigeons from park benches? How many above-average students are proliferating solely to ensure the longevity of their own alma mater? And why does it seem that one has to be a near academic dud to achieve something great?

George Mendez, a self-made man, had left Mexico for the Southwest and worked his way from ranch hand to foreman. He then bought a small herd of his own, learned bookkeeping in night school, opened a meat-packing plant and the rest is history ... but I'll continue the recitation anyway.

Mendez became a multimillionaire by age 35, a civic leader, a deacon in his church and was welcomed at his country club's poker lounge as a devoted enthusiast who played badly. But as he confided to his wealthy retired pals at the poker table one evening while losing, life wasn't all roses.

"Pals," he said, "I've been very fortunate in all ways save one. My only son – you've seen him throwing firecrackers in the swimming pool – is a bit of a scamp. He's only in grade school now, but I'm worried about his education and success in later life."

His friends, who had reason to protract Mendez's stay at the table as long as possible, commiserated with him by divulging their own family disappointments, which easily extended the game by half an hour. They talked about their dashed hopes of maintaining the family dynasty with mutterings such as "the little scalawag" and "ungrateful lout" and "They say it skips a generation" when one simply asked, "Where is he enrolled?"

Mendez was surprised. "Well, he's in sixth grade at St. Ann's Elementary."

Laughter broke out around the poker table, nearly to the point of spilling highballs.

"No, we mean what college."

"College?" Mendez was confused.

They explained the tradition in all the old-monied families across America: Parents enrolled their children at birth in private academies, preparatory schools and elite colleges, either those their own grandparents and parents had attended or better ones. "These things can't be left to chance," they declared.

"How was I to know?" Mendez asked, continuing his crafty losing-without-getting-caught information-gathering strategy.

"Your lad is young. Perhaps it is not too late," they said encouragingly. "Let's discuss it over the next several hands."

They formulated a plan, and Mendez began the application process the next week. His poker buddies made suggestions during subsequent games, helped compose the essay and wrote support letters.

To Mendez's amazement and great relief, three of the most elite schools accepted Heraldo based primarily on the letters of recommendation and the fervent essay describing him as the legacy heir of a former immigrant worker. Each school awarded him a $5,000 "incentive" scholarship (to be used to defray their $60,000 annual tuition) and begged him to visit their campus any time and enroll when he becomes eligible.

Unfortunately, when Heraldo became eligible, he was not ready. He had graduated high school with a bare minimum "C" average and approached the ivy-covered walls with great trepidation.

Yet, he was welcomed with open arms and treated to all of the charming freshman orientation activities: the picnics, skits, chapel choir performances, banquets, bonfires and meeting his don. A what? Borrowed from a bygone era, the freshman don is a faculty member assigned to interact personally and ensure that the often-disoriented youth remains in school.

Heraldo's don was Don Dr. Donald Donegal, recently retired professor emeritus, who taught one geography seminar gratis and mentored freshmen. Donegal lived only two blocks from the campus and had nothing better to do. While he resented his forced retirement at age 70 and thought the school took unfair advantage of his free mentoring services, he loved to teach and chitchat with his students.

The tweedy old fellow was disheveled but charming and loquacious with a warm smile and ever-buoyant outlook. He spent countless hours trying to motivate Heraldo to work hard and stay in school: helped with his homework, brought fraternity crib sheets, provided telling personal traits about his teachers, advised how to answer multiple-choice tests.

It was all for naught. Heraldo knew he was woefully unprepared for this school and dropped out in the middle of the term. He went to work as a junior executive in his father's business and did just fine.

The next September Heraldo began receiving the school's alumni magazine (destined always to be the first piece of mail he received whenever he moved to a new address). He got calls from perky coeds for the school's annual fund and made $500 donations. He phoned the college to say he was not really a graduate. The provost came on the line and said, "You don't need to graduate. If you are admitted to this college, once you step foot on campus, you're an alumnus."

Heraldo liked that quaint perspective. He agreed to serve on the school's environmental advisory committee and began buying all his alma mater's logo paraphernalia: the cap, muffler, reading lamp, rocking chair, grandfather clock. He attended major sports events, the alumni dinners and was named to the fund-raising committee. Looking back, he remembered his college days as some of the best years of his life.

And then he approached his father for a contribution to the school. He was persuasive, and his father agreed; the two of them would make a pledge together. But to what? After all, Heraldo admitted, he hadn't belonged to any clubs or established a major.

He liked that perspective and began buying all his alma mater's logo paraphernalia: the cap, muffler, reading lamp, rocking chair, grandfather clock.

He called his old don, Don Dr. Don, for advice, and the next year, with much fanfare at a gathering in the school chapel, the Mendez family made a $1 million donation to the emeritus professors' mentoring program.

The administrators desperately wanted the funds to endow almost any other program because they had been getting those teaching-and-advising services free. But the vice president of development had a motto: "Hook 'em today; skin 'em tomorrow." He envisioned greater Mendez gifts in the future.

So the school erected a small brick building with a comfortable conference room and half a dozen cheery offices for emeritus professors whose newly established modest stipend was matched by the college: the Dons Endowment, with Dr. Donald Donegal as chief administrator. The building was located on the edge of campus, a pleasant jaunt from Donegal's own house. By the third year, lovely ivy covered its facade as if this campus landmark had been there and would be there forever.

§

Fable 33 – Toughies

We've all heard the stories about the extremes to which some professors resort just to educate students. Most of these stories are only fables perpetrated on freshmen by upper-class students in a ritual similar to fraternity hazing. You should receive such stories with the greatest possible skepticism.

But one college professor, a Dr. Phyllis Prickelitch in the arts and letters department, maintained a legendary reputation. Of her you may believe everything.

"Dr. Migraine," as her students fondly called her, had an approach toward her subject matter, and toward teaching generally, that was almost unique. Instead of imparting a body of knowledge, she tried to force her students to think. Here are just some of the assignments she gave:

1) During the next week, determine which single book was the best ever written. This book should be so important that no college student earns a bachelor's degree without having read it thoroughly. Religious works and humor are exempt. Write a three-page paper to defend your choice.

2) Who was the greatest person who ever lived and why? Religious figures, family members and humorists are exempt, as are rock stars and sports figures.

3) What was the greatest invention of all time? Religion and knock-knock jokes are exempt, as are the wheel and the comb.

Everyone agreed Dr. Migraine was on another plane ... some said a jumbo jet, some a flying saucer. But she believed college should be a time to ponder life's meaning. She railed against any university curriculum that smacked of vocational education, and in her opinion most of them did. By her formula, all university departments named after a person, like the Seymour Snodgrass School of Biomedicine, were merely glorified vocational programs that graduated pointy headed technicians who might bumble onto a gene therapy and then endow their alma mater. Who ever heard of the Snodgrass

Dr. Prickelitch tried to force her students to think by giving assignments like: Who was the greatest person who ever lived and why?

School of Philosophy or Humanities?

Yet, because of her emphasis on thinking, many students who experienced her Introduction to Civilization 100 course vowed to change their major from hotel management or veterinary science to liberal arts and to actually secure a library card.

A likely exception was Norman Bland, a freshman from a middle-class Iowa home whose parents wanted more for their son than the boring factory jobs they held and despised. They had indoctrinated him since childhood. In answer to Dr. Migraine's essay assignment, "What flavor was the nectar of the Gods?" Norman had merely written, "Beer."

Phyllis had seen such tough cases previously. You don't last long teaching the classics if you can't cajole the obstinate or spark the vapid. She invited him to her office:

"Young man, I was quite disappointed in your recent essay and believe you can do better. What is your current major?

"Accounting. My folks want me to be an accountant."

"Why?"

"They said I'll make money and have a secure future and never get my hands dirty."

"Of course all parents want their children to be secure. What do you want?"

"The money."

"If money is your only objective, why not study to become a physician?"

"My folks say a doctor is just a highfalutin plumber, and the one with the better accountant will be richer."

"Well, how about engineering or architecture? At least those fields offer some opportunity for creative thinking."

"My math isn't that good."

"How good is your math?"

"Just good enough to be an accountant."

"Okay, but you know that accounting requires you to take three-quarters of your credits in the business school. You do realize you'll spend your entire college career studying rows of numbers."

"Yes, then I'll be an accountant."

"But a college education should be designed to expand the mind, to make you a well-rounded person, to give you an appreciation for the finer things in life."

"I'll be able to buy the finer things in life."

"Aha! How will you know what the finer things are?"

"I'll look at the price tag."

Dr. Prickelitch gave up. A lifetime of parental propaganda is too tough an act to follow. She returned to grading her class themes "What If Zeus Had Herpes?"

Near the end of the semester, much to her surprise, Mr. Bland came to her office, John Deere cap in hand.

"Dr. Prickelitch, I've thought a lot about what you said. You know I've got a good solid 'C -plus' in your class, and I really enjoy your lectures. I think I want to change majors to the classics."

"I had given up on you, Mr. Bland, but I'm delighted you changed your mind. This decision will result in a lifetime of fulfillment."

After he left her office, she placed an asterisk by his name in her grade book. It was how she rewarded those students who had seen the light, and it meant they merited a little grade inflation at the end of the semester just for encouragement.

Bland had heard about Dr. Migraine's grade bonus from fellow students. He needed that "B" in her class because he was flunking math. The ethics of his subterfuge had been a tough challenge to his Midwestern morals, but he reasoned it was better to stay in school and try math again next semester. After adding things up, he figured, "Dr. Prickelitch would be pleased I'm learning how to think for myself."

§

Fable 34 – Writing Requirement

One of the most astounding advances in higher education is a recent requirement that all college students be able to write. I should stop there because it amazes me that at some prior time writing must have been considered peripheral, like a young man's goatee. But now, apparently, writing is considered a necessity, like a young man's goatee. It is as if administrators actually believe the old dictum "writing is thinking," although the two don't even have the same number of letters.

College entry exams recently instituted a written essay portion. These are easily graded by subtracting the number of "likes," "you knows" and "I means" from 100. Yet, it seems the essays are insufficient indicators of writing ability. Universities want more proof and have added writing requirements – not in the English Department, but implanted within each major.

Placing courses such as Devising Business Plans, Scientific Journal Writing, or Composing Computer Manuals inside their associated majors awards those programs extra student headcount credit. Assigning teachers to these peripheral courses allows a department chair to sideline tenured faculty whose effectiveness in the discipline may be questionable.

Professor Euless "Glummy" Lightload taught all sections of a required junior-level engineering course. His grading had become increasingly draconian over time, and the students forced to repeat his class created a logjam in graduation rates. Concurrently, his interest in engineering had declined geometrically. He often read newspapers and paperback novels at his office desk and flipped through popular magazines in the faculty lounge.

Desperate to remove Lightload from the bottleneck class, his department chair brought him in:

"Your faculty colleagues voted you best-read in the

department, so I am naming you our new Technical Writing expert. Congratulations, you'll be teaching four sections."

Of course, as with any policy, a few unscrupulous students will try to take advantage. To them, a rule is just another challenge, as it was for Eileen Wiley, a math prodigy who struggled with language. "You're either an alpha or a numerical like me," she liked to say. It was her best witticism.

Eileen's high school English grades had kept her out of the uppity universities, and she was not about to be barred from a great graduate mathematics program. By hook and crook she managed to become a senior with a 3.8 GPA. When the graduation transcript checker brought her in for a conference, she came prepared.

"We cannot grant you a degree," Mr. Failsafe said. "You are required to have 15 hours of English, and you don't have a single credit."

"Has to be a mistake," Eileen retorted. "I got B's in every writing course I took: Menu Preparation in the Culinary College, Playbook Sketching in the Athletics Program, Calligraphy in the Art Academy, Packaging Design in the Marketing School, and Roadside Signage in the Transportation Department. Gimme my degree!"

While the university-mandated writing requirement may serve academic programs and a few devious prodigies, it is not universally embraced by all students.

Chauncey Pierpont was the son of a mining magnate. His ambition was to earn his degree in chemical engineering and immediately join his father's Wyoming bentonite conglomerate as vice president. A clever youngster, Chauncey not only aced his science subjects in high school, but as an entering university freshman, he pored over his catalogue requirements for a chemical engineering degree. He saw an easy ride through the curriculum with the possible exception of a single class: "Scientific Writing; Required for all majors."

He hoped the class dealt with writing formulas, but inquiries determined no, it was an English writing class and worse yet, it was taught by the odious Dr. Crème de la Curie, a chemist-

Dr. Curie would stand in front of the class and admonish about agreement, bellow about voice, rage about being active and fume about flow.

turned-grammarian whose students knew her facial expressions as outrage followed by exasperation followed by despair.

Because Chauncey could easily write complex chemical equations, you'd think he could master grammar. But punctuation perplexed him; he couldn't fathom how nouns and verbs differed from subjects and predicates; spelling was so arbitrary; voice, mood and tense made no sense; what was a conjunction's function; and he was sure nobody correctly used "who" and "whom" or could conjugate "lay" and "lie."

Even worse, "Dr. Curdle," as students named her after receiving their marked papers, had an acid disposition and considered her pupils the base. "These little nerds have no ear for phonics, no grasp of syntax, no feel for phraseology," she would tell her chemistry department colleagues, who wondered why Curie cared: It was only English writing.

She would stand in front of the class and admonish her students about agreement. But why? Nobody had disagreed with her. She bellowed about voice. Nobody had said a word. She raged about being active. Nobody had moved. She fumed about flow. Nobody had asked to go to the restroom.

And every semester was the same, Chauncey's sources said. Chemistry students listening to Dr. Curie's Scientific Writing lectures was like light passing through lead.

"Have you taken her class yourself?" Chauncey asked, still skeptical.

"Many times."

Chauncey realized he would never earn his degree if he had to take Scientific Writing. An unscrupulous student might have done something different, but a clever student seizes opportunity when he finds it, and Chauncey found it right there in the university curriculum catalogue. Instead of majoring, he could avoid Dr. Curie's class by minoring in chemical engineering, where Scientific Writing was not required. He would major instead in the single program in college that did not require a specific writing course.

He became an English literature major.

§

Fable 35 – The Tell

Remember the old joke about the dog who played poker? He couldn't help himself: Every time he got a good hand, he wagged his tail.

Students have an uncanny ability to pick up on the revealing signs a teacher unknowingly broadcasts. They can smell:

- fear when the novice faculty member confronts a Rose Bowl-sized lecture hall;
- confusion when the lecturer can't find his notes two minutes before the bell (of course the notes are right there in the briefcase you brought and now you're scrambling for the second time through half-graded papers, old candy bar wrappers, unpaid bills, notes for the last class, different notes for the next class, and good grief where are ... slow down, they're in there somewhere);
- panic when that jock in the back row yells, "But Mrs. Grindhard, you said you were counting 60 as the lowest 'C'";
- smugness when handing back short-answer tests where a point or two can always be shaved off each answer for "vagueness" to make sure that blonde who hasn't been to class in two weeks does not make a "B" in the course.

Students pick up on these traits. I'll tell one on myself.

For my 40th birthday present, exactly on the day itself, I got an astigmatism and needed reading glasses (it will happen to you). Now the idea of getting those little half-glasses that look so scholarly but drop down to the end of your nose did not appeal. They seemed pretentious. But with full prescription reading glasses you can't read your notes on the lectern and still police the room when you look up. Bifocals were the answer. I wore them for the next 20 years but, apparently, had the habit of taking them off and laying them on the lectern whenever I was about to tell an anecdote or lengthy story that was only tangentially related to the topic. I guess that in my mind I knew I wouldn't be needing the glasses because the anecdote was not in my notes. Students picked up on this habit and would smile broadly, lean back and put down their pens as soon as I began the rendition. I thought they enjoyed my little stories and were eagerly waiting to hear another one. Only many years later did I realize that "glasses off" meant "it won't be on the test."

I had my little "tell," but idiosyncrasy was the middle name of Perceval I. Primrose, an advertising teacher at a metropolitan community college, who seemed out of touch with the modern world. He was an anachronism, a throwback to when TV was still black and white, a hiccup in the space-time continuum.

His peculiarity was not so much his physical appearance, although he was unusually tall and rail-thin with an Adam's apple that vied for protuberance attention with his nose (his students called him "Ichabod" behind his back) and neatly coiffured mane of brown hair, his pride and joy.

Nor did his mode of dress rate as bizarre, though he was natty in his vested suits, bow tie, cuff links in his starched white dress shirts and a heavy gold watch fob that rippled across his belly as he moved. His attire was in sharp contrast with that of his students and even that of his faculty colleagues, none of whom seemed to possess a pressed shirt or to miss not having one.

No, his attitude alone made him so odd. He could not have defined it himself, would have denied it if accused, but Primrose was Old School. Some examples will illuminate:

- He could not walk into his classes without holding the door open for his female students. Neither they nor the males had a clue what he was doing. They thought he was taking attendance mentally. One fellow gave him a dollar.
- He winced when he heard "no problem" instead of "you're welcome," even from fast-food servers.
- He used a bathing cap in the shower to protect his bountiful wavy hair.
- He was so accustomed to his students wearing jeans that when a young lady wore a skirt one day, he walked over to her chair and whispered, "You don't have to attend class if you're going to a funeral."

It was not so much his appearance nor his mode of dress, but his attitude that was so odd. Primrose was Old School.

- He always tipped exactly 15 percent and kept a pocket calculator for just that purpose.
- He hated flying, not because passengers were made to feel like cattle, not because of the extra charges for baggage or seat selection, not because he was afraid, but because everybody wears sneakers, and this offended his sense of propriety for airline travel attire.
- He thought an STD was a motor oil additive.
- He had a quaint habit of sprinkling his lectures with half-finished proverbs such as "stitch in time," "bird in hand," "all that glitters" and "the best-laid schemes." His students were mystified and worried that these would be on the midterm. One of his favorites (used as a warning against tempting fate) was "won't eat pork," but he had forgotten that this was part of a quip he had heard from a Jewish friend in his NYC advertising office 10 years before, the full statement being, "Even a rabbi who becomes an atheist won't eat pork on Yom Kippur."

Primrose's students caught on quickly enough to play his quirks to their advantage.

"Sir," one would ask in class, "When you asked on the test 'What was the best political slogan of all time,' a bunch of us answered 'I Like Ike,' and you counted it wrong."

Primrose didn't recall having used that example, but hearing it aloud he agreed it was his favorite. He would count it right.

Students wrote their term papers on nostalgic ad campaigns from the 1950s and 1960s. They had heard from others that you couldn't go wrong with the Marlboro Man or Pepsodent or Firestone "where the rubber meets the road."

One creative student searched the Internet and made a CD of Broadway show tunes that she played just loud enough from under her chair in the front row. Primrose found himself humming. Unable to concentrate, he dismissed the class early.

They kept him from covering additional chapters by cruelly leading him off-topic with simple queries such as "What actor played The Jolly Green Giant?" and spent an entire class session searching for a shorter slogan than "Coke Is It." (Somebody suggested a tag line for a company offering to improve credit score ratings: "Up Yours." Primrose was effusive about the punchy phrase and baffled by their uncontrollable laughter.)

They embarrassed him by asking about ads for feminine hygiene products, contraceptives and Victoria's Secret.

And they discovered his tell. Whenever he was about to mention something that would be on the next test, he absentmindedly ran his fingers through his immaculately styled hair making it stick out. On days he tried to catch up before the next test, by the time he left class his hair would be a mess. "How did that happen?" he wondered when straightening his bow tie in the men's room.

"How did this happen?" his department chair asked.

"How did what happen?"

The chair pushed a printout of Primrose's semester grades across the table.

"How did 95 percent of your students manage to make A's in your Intro to Advertising class?" he queried with icy enmity. "You might get away with such tomfoolery (Primrose liked the word but not where this was going) at a snooty school, but this ain't Princeton and your students ain't princes. What's up?"

"I don't know what happened. Halfway through the semester," he brushed through his hair, "they got smarter," another brush. Maybe I'm just a good teacher," brush, brush.

"Are you keeping something from me?" his chair asked.

"Okay, from the third week forward nearly all my students got every test question right and they kept doing it the entire term."

His department chair smiled. "I think I can help."

The next semester saw a complete turnaround. Oh, his students still led him off-topic, played show tunes and embarrassed him with salacious questions, but the grades he turned in formed a perfect bell-shaped curve with a mean of 72. And he was becoming accustomed to his new look: A closely shaven bald head went well with his natty attire and Old School attitude. His students called him "Daddy Warbucks" behind his back.

§

Fable 36 – Arrogance, part 1

They say absolute power corrupts absolutely, and while I have come to accept that corruption may be inevitable, it's the arrogance I find so off-putting. Not that I was always such a purist. I'll share an early experience that should have been a warning to me about power and arrogance.

It was the arrival evening prior to the August basic training rotation at Ft. Polk, Louisiana. After being issued all the clothing and gear we could carry, about 20 recruits were assigned to a temporary barracks for the night. Before leaving us, the sergeant asked if anybody had R.O.T.C.

"I had two years in high school."

"You're the barracks orderly for the night," he said and left me a sheet of instructions.

Don't think I was a stranger to wielding authority. I had been deputy captain of our class baseball team in the fifth grade, among other positions. But something about this commission triggered my ego as I read the dozen instruction points to the men. The first required keeping barracks guard duty throughout the night in case of fire or similar calamity; failure meant the stockade. Other instructions dealt with recognizing a fire or similar calamity, and leading the men to safety. However, one instruction required that each sentry wear a heavy, rubberized raincoat and rubber wide-brimmed hat. I organized drawing straws to determine the guards and hours, and the first guy put on his poncho and hat at 10 p.m. and sat on his footlocker. He looked silly and uncomfortable as sweat began trickling down his face almost immediately.

Hell hath no fury like an August night in Ft. Polk, except maybe a July night. At 10:30, the guy gasped aloud, "I can't take it," and threw off the soaking poncho and hat. A discussion ensued among the four other men who drew the short straws. But I was in charge, and I remained adamant that the rubber outfits must be worn.

At 10:30 p.m., the sentry gasped aloud, "I can't take it," and threw off the soaking poncho and hat. A discussion ensued.

Then all five turned on me.

"It's a stupid rule," said the group, surrounding me menacingly.

Mutiny! A direct challenge to my authority as group leader that could not be tolerated.

"The instructions say …."

"We don't care."

"I'm in charge here, and I say you must …."

"We will rip off your limbs and stomp on the pieces," they said, or words to that effect.

"Okay, but it's the stockade for you if you get caught," I retorted and went back to my bunk red faced and fuming.

When I awoke at 3 a.m., I noticed the first sentry was still on his footlocker in his undershorts sound asleep.

I should have learned a valuable life lesson then, but in later power positions I was no less arrogant than were most academic administrators I knew.

Take Provost Clara "Cheeky" Clabberwaith, the soles of whose shoes were permanently indented by the bumps of her colleagues' vertebrae. The time was mid-December, just halfway through the last recession, which decreased state academic budgets 12 percent. Such ruthless budget cuts decimate universities because the vast majority of expenses are for tenured faculty, whose continued employment is sacrosanct. Additionally, unlike businesses, most universities operate on "zero-based budgets." That means any operating funds that remain at the end of each fiscal year are wiped out, and that means there are no carryover reserve funds that might help an administrator out of a tough jam like a 12 percent budget cut.

"Hope we didn't keep you from something important," Clabberwaith intoned glibly as the Liberal Arts dean entered the conference room two minutes late, "but we need to discuss the operating budget, if you have time."

She scowled individually at the deans gathered around the huge oblong table. "These budget cuts are too severe to get by on the usual methods of doing without travel, equipment, supplies, repairs, adjuncts, secretaries, janitors and the other incidentals ... yes, Bob?"

Dean Robert Dealing, one of her favorites, smiled and said, "We in the Business School got it covered from the Dean's Discretionary Fund. Have a profitable holiday season," and he exited the room.

Dean Nancy Sturgeon, Clabberwaith's other favorite, stood and said, "The Medical School will postpone constructing its new MRI suite for six months. Stay well," and she left the room.

"That leaves the rest of you paupers," Clabberwaith said with a snide chortle. "I believe program cuts is the only way you can pay what you owe, and it's about time."

The specter of cutting academic programs is the kiss of death for a dean. Sure, it might work surreptitiously over a decade, but a sword-slashing cut is certain to unite faculty, students and alumni in a hopping mad frenzy that usually results in the dean being sent back to classroom teaching with a sword-slashed salary.

"Dr. Clabberwaith," the dean of Education said, "we would be required to spend the same amount of money teaching those who remain enrolled in our existing degree programs."

"True. Still, you could combine all your elementary and secondary education courses. Nobody would notice."

"But Dr. Clabberwaith," the dean of Sciences protested, "how can you combine geology with earth sciences or merge genetics with biology?"

"I could do it in a heartbeat," she sneered.

"Dr. Clabberwaith," the dean of the Media Arts College complained, "the television faculty don't get along with those in print journalism, theater hates speech, and nobody likes the geeks in digital graphics."

"I'm thinking about calling them all 'communications' and moving them as a group into Liberal Arts," the provost said with a smirk.

"Not another department!" the Liberal Arts dean exclaimed. "We're already two-thirds of the university and we can't make ends meet now."

"Ah, yes. Your bloated bailiwick is a shambles. But you could easily cut costs by eliminating just the departments whose faculty outnumber student majors, or the ones that don't really meet academic standards."

"Which programs are those?"

"I will gladly share the list I've been keeping," she replied callously.

"This is unacceptable," the deans said in unison.

"Then we can do it the old fashioned way," the provost snapped back.

"What way is that?"

"I cut every dean's budget by 12 percent, and you can fight it out face-to-face with your department chairs without the slightest regard for program quality, just like always." Clabberwaith picked up her notes and sauntered out of the room.

She was a haughty one alright, but the king of arrogance has to be a college president I once knew at a deep-South university. This divulgence comes so close to truth that I simply must use an alias but, with compassion and sensitivity, I will do everything in my power not to call him "Bubba." I'll pause here to think of an appropriate substitute name.

§

Fable 37 – Arrogance, part 2

I was searching for a fitting pseudonym to call a deep-South university president I knew who was perhaps the emperor of arrogance, but I had vowed not to call him "Bubba" out of kindness and deference to his office.

So he was President Goober "Redneck" Hayseed, who was said to have been hired to this emerging Southern school from a phone booth one rainy day after serving a stint as a young high school principal in a hamlet just within state borders. His master's in education administration brought him in as department chair, and after getting a diploma mill doctorate, he became dean. Then, a former high school student Goober had helped secure a football scholarship was elected governor and appointed Goober the university's president.

There's an epigram warning against challenging the really powerful: "Never pick a fight with anyone who buys ink by the barrel." Well, Goober began making his own appointments, and soon the entire central administration was a good-old-boy network of former fishing and drinking buddies from the distant little village and its environs. The vice president of finance was his former insurance salesman; the academic vice president had managed the town's bookstore; the football coach had been the high school varsity coach; the vice president of public relations had been editor of the tiny weekly newspaper, and so forth. They formed a tight-knit cadre in support of every pompous decision Goober made:

- Obstinate faculty members got themselves reassigned from the main campus to a satellite campus 125 miles away in a lumber mill town. "It's our way or the Interstate," Goober told them. "Kiss your family goodbye."
- Real trouble makers landed at the university's international sister campus. (I have a theory that you can tell the status of any U.S. university by drawing mile-wide concentric circles centered on the most fashionable district in the world's poshest

capitals. I haven't looked it up, but I bet Harvard has a sister campus within one mile of the ritziest zone in Paris.) Goober's sister campus was a lean-to in a remote area of Sri Lanka. "You get a going-away present," he'd tell the trouble makers, "A free leprosy inoculation. Write while you can."

• One of his buddies had gotten a sales job with a big computer firm and convinced Goober to centralize all university records on a massive computer system. That was eight years ago, and after investments approaching $20 million, it still didn't work. In fact, it was those commitments that had kept faculty and staff at 1.5 percent raises when they got any raises at all.

The computer firm sponsored the annual administrators' retreat. This was a 10-day, all-expense-paid trip to the best golfing spas in a four-state area. The trip was planned by one of Goober's full-time secretaries, hired for that job alone, and involved such intricate and lavish planning that the driver of the trailer truck transporting the golf carts returned with enough terry cloth bathrobes to complete his Christmas giving list.

But all this was just business as usual. What took place behind the scenes was really arrogant.

Each new sports season brought "Fantasy Fever" where the Good Old Boys formed their fantasy football, basketball, hockey or baseball teams by bartering university resources (amenities like travel or equipment funds) for outstanding players and betting against one another in a winner-take-all pool. Their team-building strategy took a lot of time, but the GOBs were passionate players and never let mundane university business interfere with such serious pursuits. "Signing off on faculty grant applications and interviewing job candidates can wait," they scoffed. "There's always a new round next year."

Rather than asking the legislature for a desperately needed classroom building, Goober instead got a new health complex with the latest gym equipment, racket ball and tennis courts, indoor track, Olympic pool and a very plush administrators' lounge. Faculty, staff and students were charged annual fees to use the complex. "Any halfwit knows it must be self-sustaining," Goober answered contemptuously. "How else would we retire

Real trouble makers landed at the university's international sister campus. "You get a going-away present," he'd tell them.

the bonds?"

When department chairs complained that roof leaks had closed classrooms, and students were dodging falling ceiling panels in the hallways, Goober announced an addition to the football stadium. Asked if a third-rate football program with more participants on the field than attendance in the stands merited such an investment, Goober shot a callous glare.

"Only a jackass would ask such a question," he snarled. "You can't expect to have a winning season without a skybox where administrators can entertain potential donors."

And it went on like this for years, until the same recession that Provost Clabberwaith used to lambaste her deans caught Goober in a financial squeeze. He had authorized no raises, froze all hiring, increased teaching loads across the board, cancelled adjunct contracts, sacked secretaries (not the vacation planner), stopped having grass cut on campus and turned off the heater in the Olympic swimming pool (not in the administrators' spa). But as the end of the fiscal year neared he still had $20,000 in his operating fund to spend (see "zero-based budgets"). It was a close decision. He could rehire the elderly secretary who was featured on the local evening news when her house was foreclosed and she was diagnosed with a terminal illness. Instead he bought a shiny new desk for his office, "a real humdinger," he gloated.

At this point I must make a little "arrogance aside":

There once was a college basketball coach whose team consistently won Sweet Sixteen championships. He was the hero of the campus, the pride of the city and a regional media celebrity. His bonuses netted him twice what an orthodontist earns; he signed autographs and ate free at the finest restaurants. Eager parents fought to have their 9-year-olds attend his summer basketball camp at $3,000 a head. But then it was reported that he had used substantial alumni donor funds to attract his star players; received a new "loaner" Escalade every year from the local Cadillac dealer, which he later sold; and had been betting on college basketball games with a Las Vegas bookie. Community feelings were mixed. Should the college stand behind him or give him up to the district attorney? And then it was reported that he charged his summer basketball camp kids $1 each for an eight-ounce Pepsi in a paper cup. That did it; he went to jail. Enough said.

What was Goober's penalty for buying that shiny new desk? The faculty were outraged and voted overwhelmingly to establish a campus-wide Teachers' Union. The GOBs were aghast. The time it would take to haggle with those malcontents would seriously jeopardize their own success during Fantasy Fever. The computer company contract would come under scrutiny and endanger their annual administrators' retreat. Their authority to run the university just as they pleased might be questioned.

All of this came to pass the first year the Union tried to flex its muscles, and I'd like to be able to tell you that Goober and his cohorts got their comeuppance, that the board of trustees fired them all, that the Union forced them to change their arrogant ways, that they hightailed it back to their rural hamlet in shame and remorse. I'd like to be able to say that, but it seems those who attain a high enough position of power usually win.

After the first year's minor setbacks, Goober and his GOBs ignored the Union representatives entirely, turned the negotiations over to their team of full-time university attorneys, and quickly regressed to their usual arrogant ways. Maybe the suitable exhortation here is: Never pick a fight with anyone who retains lawyers by the dozen.

§